VISITING
THE PAST

*a guide to finding and understanding
Britain's archaeology*

D1634891

Reading Borough Council

3412601035861 5

VISITING THE PAST

a guide to finding and understanding Britain's archaeology

GILLIAN HOVELL

The History Press

READING BOROUGH LIBRARIES

Askews	
936.1	£12.99

Front cover: Carreg Samson in Pembrokeshire (© Gillian Hovell)
Back cover, clockwise from top left:
Hadrian's Wall (© Gillian Hovell);
Bryn Celli Ddu (© Gillian Hovell);
Devil's Arrow, Boroughbridge (© Gillian Hovell);
Ironbridge (© Andrew Hovell);
Ironbridge blast furnace (© Andrew Hovell)

First published 2009

The History Press
The Mill, Brimscombe Port
Stroud, Gloucestershire, GL5 2QG
www.thehistorypress.co.uk

© Gillian Hovell, 2009

The right of Gillian Hovell to be identified as the Author
of this work has been asserted in accordance with the
Copyrights, Designs and Patents Act 1988.

All rights reserved. No part of this book may be reprinted
or reproduced or utilised in any form or by any electronic,
mechanical or other means, now known or hereafter invented,
including photocopying and recording, or in any information
storage or retrieval system, without the permission in writing
from the Publishers.

British Library Cataloguing in Publication Data.
A catalogue record for this book is available from the British Library.

ISBN 978 0 7524 4833 6

Typesetting and origination by The History Press
Printed in Great Britain

CONTENTS

ACKNOWLEDGEMENTS

An archaeology guide is like reading a detective novel. You get to know the settings and the characters involved and then you start to piece together who did what, when and how. And, like murder mystery tales, the best final denouements are gained when you get help and information from many different sources and witnesses. Writing an archaeology book is no different – the weaving together of its many threads into a coherent story is the result of support and guidance from many people.

In the first instance, my thanks go to professional archaeologist Kevin Cale for his unflagging work in enabling and guiding the many community archaeology projects in the Nidderdale area. Without his input and his teaching, and indeed his patience as he coped with my foolish questions, I would never have even started down the happy and satisfying road to archaeology.

In a similar vein, my eternal thanks go to my very dear friends Jim Brophy and Michael Thorman – to whom this book is dedicated – for regularly braving the elements and my company on any number of windswept hillsides and for making archaeology such fun. Even in horizontal rain and boggy fields we never fell out – instead we just fell about when I fell in. Archaeology is at its best when it's not a lone pastime – so, to our members and friends in our Iron-Age (Nidderdale) project and to Norman Bradley and his family for letting us play in your fields, not forgetting those in all the other Community Archaeology Groups who have welcomed me into their midst over the years, my thanks.

I would never have got even that far without the unstinting encouragement from certain special folk in my formative years long ago: 'Mrs Jones' who read *Tales of Greece and Rome* to me when I was nine and started this whole fascination; Ros Hall (née Brown) who encouraged me, sharing an early enthusiasm for all things classical and quietly feeding an obsession that often seemed like madness to others; and my tutors at Exeter University, David Harvey and Professor Peter Wiseman in particular, who inspired my continuing love of ancient history. On the writing side, I owe a debt of gratitude to so many: to Alex Gazzola for all his support and encouragement as I started out on this enterprise; to Samantha Parker for nudging me into the world of websites and PR; to my army of proofreaders, Andrew Hovell, Jim Brophy and Michael Thorman, who scoured the manuscript for me and who were so generous with their time; and to Liz Forrest who did all that and also generously shared her substantial knowledge of all things Scottish; to Wendy Logue and Miranda Embleton-Smith at The History Press for guiding me through the practicalities of it all, and to all the team there. In particular my editor Fran Cantillion for keeping me on the straight and narrow.

A special mention must go to Liz Forrest and my husband, Andrew, for scouring both the country and their albums for the best photographic shots, and to the individuals and organisations who have generously allowed the use of their wonderful images: Alan Ball and Andrew Horeckyj; Jim Brophy; Janis Heward; Helen and Mark Hovell; Archaeolink Prehistory Park; the Bronze Age Re-enactment company; Chaldon church, Kent Archaeological Rescue Unit (for Dover's Painted Roman House); the Ermine Street Guard; the Great Orme Mines; the Fair Isles Medieval Society; the incumbent and churchwardens of St Mary the Virgin at Iffley; Isbister's Tomb of the Eagles; the Old Palace School of John Whitgift; Palmerston Forts Society; Vikings! Of Middle England; the Vindolanda Trust; the Weald and Downland Open Air Museum and the York Archaeological Trust (Hungate Dig).

This book would not exist without my friends who cheered me on (yes, Annie Mitchell, that includes you) and my family, Andrew, Helen and Mark who continued to believe in me and put up with my months of scribbling and tapping away in solitude. You indulged me as we repeatedly visited yet another archaeological ruin and squeezed in yet another detour to an ancient site – thank you for smiling as you asked, as we set out on an inevitable walk while on holiday, 'so tell us now: is the archaeology at the beginning, the middle or the end of this walk we're going on?'. It was, of course, at all three points.

Gillian Hovell
July 2009

INTRODUCTION

Welcome to the story of Britain. It's a tale we've heard many times and in many ways but this time it's personal. This is history we can reach out to and touch for ourselves: it's all around us, etched on our hillsides and filling our valleys. This is a journey to places you thought you knew, but with this book as a guide, you'll have a new map to explore them with and a fresh viewpoint to see them from.

So just where are we going? Our route starts in the long-deserted homes of our prehistoric dawn. Soon it reaches the enigmatic standing stones, earthy mounds and stony-faced fortresses that once dominated the country. On our way we shall encounter generations of fresh settlers with new ideas and witness countless lives that shaped our countryside. We shall move on, through the belching power of industry as it forged its way across our landscape, until we pause at the battle-scarred land of the World Wars. Our journey will take us across the length and breadth of Britain and through the millennia from mankind's first steps on our soil to our own personal yesterdays.

This narrative of our islands is told through archaeology, that is, the physical remains left behind by our ancestors. Some of the ruins in our story are monumental and obvious: take Stonehenge for example. We may not know everything there is to

Stonehenge is an obvious example of British archaeology. (©The History Press Ltd)

know about it, but it's prehistoric, well-visited and pretty unmissable as monuments go.

While grand sites like Stonehenge make for great days out, if we look at them more closely – as archaeology – they can do so much more than simply entertain us for a few hours. A visit to an archaeological site is a visit into the past: every monument, every ruin and every sacred site tells a story. And even the very bones of our ancestors can paint a vivid picture for us of what their lives were like, if only we know where to look.

This book aims to share archaeology's hidden clues and to help to unlock the secrets of our monuments, whether they be large or small, unimaginably ancient or more recent and numbingly familiar. World famous heritage sites and previously barely-noticed lumps in anonymous fields all have their tales to tell. So who is this book for? If you're a complete novice, a TV history fan or a practised amateur archaeologist, then this book is for you. If you enjoy walks in the country or like seeing a new point of view, then getting to grips with our islands' archaeology is for you. All you need is reasonable eyesight, some sound footwear and a good dollop of curiosity. Take this book with you as you get out and explore Britain's archaeology for yourself: see the great sites in a new light, or pop out for a local stroll and discover just how much silent history lurks around every corner.

First though, settle down to a little armchair travelling. Read on and discover how to visit the past and bring yesterday's stories into our lives today.

PART ONE

Getting Started

WHAT IS ARCHAEOLOGY?

Let's begin with that most basic question: what is archaeology? What do we think of when we talk of archaeology? Our first thoughts may be of vast ruins of conquering empires, hoards of treasure salvaged from the earth or muddy holes in the ground surrounded by even muddier diggers (*colour plate 1*). These are the aspects of archaeology that dominate our screens and (very rarely) our news.

Yet there is another, far more intimate, side to archaeology. That field at the end of your road, the building we work in or walk past every day and the hill that dominates the landscape may all contain a slice of history. Many people are surprised to discover that our lives are surrounded by archaeology. Even though we all live cheek by jowl with it, we rarely notice it. I hope to share how archaeology (and the history it reveals) is as much a part of our lives as the buildings we call home and the roads we travel on today.

Of course, organic material usually decays and so all we are left with are just the stones, shadows of postholes and a few artefacts such as pottery and metallic tools. It's rather like being asked to describe a finished 5000-piece jigsaw having been given no picture and fewer than fifty pieces in total. Yet that can be enough to know if your jigsaw is trying to recreate a photograph or a painting, a natural scene or an indoor scene, a human environment or a lunar landscape – you can get a general impression of the picture. And, in the same way, those tiny archaeological clues can tell us much more than you might imagine.

Today, there are many ways to examine those clues. Indeed, one of the fascinations of archaeology is that it is a multi-skilled discipline which opens the mind to evidence from all angles: laboratory analysis, fieldwork surveys on and under the ground or in rivers and lakes or under the sea; anthropological studies of present-day primitive cultures; gory forensic science on long-dead bodies; reconstructive experimental archaeology … the list goes on. But there is one skill which everyone can possess and which doesn't require expensive kit, a science degree or a silly hat and a trowel.

The shape of this bump in the ground tells us that it may be a 5000 year-old burial mound. (© Gillian Hovell)

That skill is typography, otherwise known as identifying artefacts and features from their particular style and shape. And it is this aspect of archaeology that this book concentrates on.

It is possible to recognise the probable age of a flint tool by its chunkiness or its size; we can spot potential burial mound dates by their shape, size and site; we can identify the various possible ages of parts of a church by their architectural styles; and we can discover a likely Roman fort by the shape and layout of a few lumps in the ground. Obviously we cannot discover everything about an historic site simply by looking at it: excavation, analyses and the study of relevant historical documents are just some of the other elements which need to combine to tell us the true story. But it is a great starting point and, combined with just enough historical know-how, we can all use it to begin to 'read' the landscape and monuments around us.

ARCHAEOLOGY MATTERS

But why should we bother with the splintered ruins and fragmented remains that litter our landscape? Many would claim they matter because they are our heritage – and that makes us who we are today. Others would say they are precious because they are priceless and unique: a burial mound built 4000 years ago can never be replaced once lost. Both are absolutely right, but we should add and never dismiss another, often forgotten, reason for treasuring our relics of the past – millions of us subconsciously acknowledge it when we take the family on a day out to a famous castle or walk the dog at the local abbey ruins. We instinctively do it because it's fun and it feels good. It is no coincidence that some of our greatest tourist attractions are historic monuments – there is a basic and primeval satisfaction in rubbing shoulders with our ancestral roots (*colour plate 2*).

However, it is possible to take it a step further. Instead of simply mingling in an anonymous crowd of historical features, we can get to know them. Seeing those ruins from the past in a fresh, new way is thrilling – when we know what we're looking at, a walk in the countryside becomes a personal trip through time as we pass a previously unremarked medieval field boundary, a trace of an Iron Age hut circle or a church which glories in centuries of alterations and additions. After reading this book you may never go for a walk and simply admire the view again – history will accompany you all the way.

Personally, my own addiction to history began at the tender age of nine when a teacher called Mrs Jones breathlessly read to us from a slender blue volume that was just packed with stories from another time and a distant world. As I sat spellbound, I saw the world in a new, previously unimagined way: the tales of the past were full of people living in different circumstances and often obeying different social rules and yet they were *just like us*. I realised that life can be different but familiar at the same time and I came to realise that, by comparing our lives with those of others, we can see ourselves anew as part of one timeless family of humanity. Mrs Jones may have been reading the *Tales of Greece and Rome* but the same principle applies to any era in any country.

Now, decades later, I relish the days I can spend unearthing fresh traces of our history while leading a local community archaeology project and I simply cannot imagine a world without the thread of history running through it – it would be like trying to paint a picture of the present without having any canvas to work on – you would end up with nothing more than a sloppy, shapeless and globby mess on the carpet.

This book is designed to be that canvas, a basic tool on which you can add whatever tints and shades of history you come across. I want to share with you that adventure of discovery, that increasing awareness that we are a living part of a coherent and ever-continuing story: by opening our eyes and really looking at the spaces we live and work in today, we can catch a glimpse of what it was like to be a person just like ourselves here in this place but in another time. For archaeology concerns the most fundamental topic of all – human life. It unearths echoes of past lives, of locals who worked and loved here day in, day out, and who died here too: the peasant tilling the heavy soil, the soldier of the ranks on lookout from the castle wall, the weary monk stumbling to matins. We walk where they walked before us – we share their space, if not their time. Just sometimes it is the dignitary, the politician or the king who tramped the fields and the stone-flagged floor, and they may have funded the building of monuments, castles and abbeys and probably visited them and feasted in splendour. But more often it is the stonemason patiently carving the block, the servant scurrying to serve the master, or the farmer scraping a living from his small enclosure whose living space we share by visiting the past. *Doctor Who* can transport us to other imagined times but archaeology is the nearest we can get to real time travel.

Archaeology aims to understand the past, but in doing so it also makes sense of the present. For that past created our present and we cannot know nor understand where we are going unless we know where we are coming from.

St Margaret's church in Hales, Norfolk, takes us back 800 years to the time when the Normans ruled the land. Typical Norman details include the rounded apse. (© Andrew Hovell)

And archaeology is not just the discovery of the material remains of the past but the interpretation of how, why and when folk did what they did and made what they made – and, because human nature never changes, it can tell us how, why and when folk are inspired to do things nowadays or even in the future. At a fundamental level therefore, archaeology tells us much about what makes us human. In fact, because it is the sole evidence for our prehistoric past, it is archaeology that provides our understanding of where all modern people came from and how our early societies developed. Archaeology is therefore crucial to the discovery and interpretation of our roots.

Some ages (especially those early millennia) have left behind very little evidence. Every find counts. Each one offers a unique flickering glimpse of a lost moment of time: the charred remains of a meal cooked over a particular fire on a particular day; a life lost to a flint arrowhead between the ribs; even a letter home for more socks from a Roman soldier on the frontier of his world. And, because even a slightest flicker can change the focus of a picture, so can a single find tweak our view of history and therefore our understanding of our heritage. This is part of the fun of archaeology – it is not a static, fixed science, but a continuing voyage of discovery. The bickering television archaeologists aren't just arguing in order to make a more entertaining programme, they are comparing and disputing their latest theories – and archaeology actually thrives on this controversy and debate because new finds and new theories open our eyes to fresh interpretations and ideas.

We all need to be aware that any and every find could help to write a fresh page in the history books. Any new find should therefore be shared with the central recorders of our islands' history, the Heritage Offices and the Portable Antiquities Scheme (PAS). Even a quick peek at the images on the PAS's website, www.findsdatabase.org, soon reveals how a single find adds material to an ever-growing and fascinating story.

So it all matters. But let's climb down off the soapbox and remember that archaeology has many personal benefits: it gets you out in the fresh air; it's good exercise (physically and mentally); it can be sociable and exciting, even entertaining; and it gives you a whole new perspective on the world. But, most of all, it's fun, and anyone can do it.

MONUMENTAL HISTORY

Where should we start? We need to begin by recognising the different ages in Britain's history. There's a timeline to help us in Part Two, but the briefest of summaries goes something like this: prehistoric folk in Britain eventually settled down; various opportunistic people poured in, including the Romans, followed by church missionaries, Angles, Saxons and then the Vikings and finally the Normans in 1066, who kicked off the medieval period with bureaucracy and abbeys and castles galore. By 1500, the first glimmerings of a modern age can be glimpsed in a post-medieval era which grew into the industrial age and life as we now know it.

That's several thousand years in a nutshell, but how do we zoom in for a closer look at them?

To get a feel for any one era, pop into a museum dedicated to that age – several are listed in Part Two. If you happen to be in England's capital, an afternoon's stroll around the British Museum is an excellent taster for all the eras. Head for the European galleries and see some of the major discoveries unearthed in Britain: prehistoric burial goods, the Sutton Hoo riches, the chariot wheel from a northern cart burial, Roman finds galore … undoubtedly though, the best places to get to grips with these ages are the sites themselves. Start with those we are vaguely familiar with and which obviously belong to set eras in history: the distinctly prehistoric monuments or the grand Roman villas and forts; the early Christian communities or the later ruined medieval abbeys and castles which are so much a part of our modern image of the countryside; or maybe the still solid foundations of the industrial age. Each era in our history has its share of these atmospheric and enlightening places, and the pick of the best of them is also set out in Part Two.

We are incredibly fortunate in Britain to have a vast wealth of excellent sites to visit. Fantastic places of real historic interest are restored, maintained and presented to us by national organisations such as English Heritage, Historic Scotland, Wales' CADW, and the National Trust for England and Scotland, private trusts, professional archaeologists, land owners, lifelong devotees of particular sites, a vast and countless army of dedicated volunteers and even, dare I say it, the government. Regrettably, this single book cannot hope to do justice to all the sites, for each and every one of them could fill several books on their own merit, such is the historical worth of each site. However, what we can sample is the breadth and depth of Britain's archaeology. First of all, there are the big, well-maintained, signboard-filled sites, complete with their tours and guidebooks. They range from the Tudor warship, the *Mary Rose*, sunk 500 years ago in the Solent off the south coast, to the ancient stone towers called brochs which defended the rocky northern shores of Scotland. Other monuments of every kind from prehistory right through to the Second World War are less publicised but quietly stand guard on every shore and punctuate every region. Then there are the archaeological sites made famous by their finds rather than by their visual impact. Ancient, rich, princely graves, such as the Amesbury Archer's, the cart burials and Sutton Hoo are splendid examples.

Castle Acre in Norfolk is a classic medieval castle. (© Andrew Hovell)

Ongoing excavations, like these at Hungate can be visited and even taken part in. (© York Archaeological Trust, Hungate Dig)

Some major sites have ongoing research programmes and excavations where active archaeology is still visibly continuing and regularly brings new information to light. The Bronze Age Flag Fen site in Cambridgeshire, the Roman fort at Vindolanda where the unique writing tablets were found and the Viking Hungate dig in York are just a few examples where you can see present-day archaeology in action. Peering at the actual artefacts, hearing about the way they were found and maybe even meeting some of the people involved in their unearthing is an inspiring and enriching experience.

Other sites were excavated decades ago, but are now enjoying the status of established tourist attractions, Stonehenge being an obvious example. Many other sites, such as medieval castles like Beaumaris on Anglesey and Roman sites such as Housesteads Fort on Hadrian's Wall are justified in attracting thousands of visitors a year. When visiting such places, it's easy to get caught up in the throng and swept around at camera-snap speed, but it's well worth pausing a while longer and taking a closer look. Traipsing around along the guidebook's tour is one excellent option but another is more dynamic and rewarding: get up close and get familiar with the site – notice the special, interesting bits that stand out. And, as you visit more archaeological sites, regular features soon become familiar: the long barrows and round barrows of prehistoric ritual landscapes separate into distinct markers for different eras; the hypocausts that provided underfloor heating rapidly become an unmistakably Roman construction; and the first floor entrance to medieval fort towers become a familiar set piece. Soon the features that represent particular eras, from Roman mosaic styles to rounded Norman or pointed Gothic church windows, all become clues to the age of the site.

UNRAVELLING THE PAST

Of course, it is crucial to realise that life isn't always that easy. Different eras do not inhabit distinctly different areas and there are many multi-phased archaeological sites in Britain. You can't often simply say 'this is a Bronze Age landscape here, but over there on that hill is a Iron Age landscape and ne'er the twain shall meet' because people simply do not, and did not, live like that: Iron Age folk would have reused already ancient sites just as we continue to live in villages that were once medieval and bits of the modern A5 roars along above the ancient Roman Watling Street.

The key point here is that each generation uses the land and buildings or sites around them for their own purposes and Stonehenge serves as a dramatic example of this.

New theories regarding Stonehenge crop up with the regularity of dandelions on a lawn as new, advanced investigations unearth fresh evidence but, as far as we can tell, as early as c.8000 BC, there was an early Middle Stone Age (Mesolithic) timber structure near the present-day site of the monument. Then, in about 3500 BC, long barrows were built to house burials and a causewayed enclosure was constructed and two ritual stone-lined avenues ('cursus' monuments) were added by the end of the millennium.

Excavations and analysis tell us that Stonehenge's history is mind-blowingly complex, covering thousands of years: a bank and ditch containing a timber henge was added in the Neolithic Age, then a horseshoe of the Preseli 'bluestones' was built before being rearranged inside the famous massive sarsen stones. An earthwork avenue was eventually added in the Bronze Age and round burial mounds sprouted all around it. It has taken decades of skilled digging and science to unravel Stonehenge's story. And yet, even in this most complicated of sites we can simply stand and look to see the distinct long barrows, causewayed enclosure and avenues which are still visible today – and these virtual flagship markers of a New Stone Age (Neolithic) 'ritual landscape' enable an informed guess that this was a lively ritual site in the Neolithic, over 5000 years ago. Meanwhile, the round burial mounds tell us that it was still important 1000 years later in the Bronze Age.

So, whether it's a large and famous site like Stonehenge or just an anonymous mound in a field near you, archaeology often has distinct features that tell us how old it might be and to which age it probably belongs. But just where can we find those tell-tale links with the past?

SPOTTING HIDDEN ARCHAEOLOGY

In an age of expensive leisure activities and extortionate family days out, archaeology-spotting is a refreshingly cost-free hobby. It is true that some of the great and the good, like Rievaulx Abbey in Yorkshire and Orkney's Skara Brae, charge us to visit them – and rightly so, because you cannot maintain such sites without substantial funding. But many of our impressive sites are absolutely free to visit, being funded and cared for by national schemes: prehistoric forts like Mam Tor sit on public hillsides and stone circles loom out of the landscape as you walk on bleak open spaces like Bodmin Moor, while Roman ruins like Silchester's town walls, deserted medieval villages like Wharram Percy, and stumps of castles litter our countryside and have free open access granted to them.

However, these are the official sites. There is another side to archaeology. There are countless archaeological features throughout Britain that are humble and, despite being remarkable, are often ignored. They have no guides and no signboard. They have survived, not because of a grant or sponsorship, but simply because they are out in the open countryside, where they have been left unnoticed and in peace, unsmothered by new buildings and prey only to the elements. There are literally thousands of these modest tumbledown ruins and grassy lumps and bumps which never get into any of the guidebooks. Every one of them is archaeology with its own tale to tell, and this modest archaeology beneath our feet peers at us from the unlikeliest of places.

To get the best out of a walk through history, don't just admire the view, get into the habit of looking out for a number of tell-tale archaeology clues:

◉ LOOK OUT FOR . . .

- ◉ **Crop marks** – Made by crops growing higher over in-filled ditches and shorter over buried wall foundations. Is there a pattern to them? Are they in a line (an old wall?) or are they square (and old building or fort?) or circular (a roundhouse or burial mound maybe?)
- ◉ **Walls** – Are there abrupt changes in style showing different build dates or blocked-in gateways where a track once passed through?
- ◉ **Fields** – Are any very different in shape to the others around it? Are they modern and square, like a patchwork quilt, or ancient and round or wriggly? Ancient stubby, decaying field walls on a deserted, high moorland may be prehistoric and low stony wall foundations around small fields could be medieval (*colour plate 3*).
- ◉ **Molehills and rabbit scratchings** – Check for pottery, flint, charcoal or other materials.
- ◉ **Flat circular or rectangular platforms in lumpy fields** – Was there a building here?
- ◉ **Dark or light patches in ploughed soil** – Is there something like slag (iron-working refuse) scattered here?

Blocked gateways in walls hint at old trackways that once went this way.
(© Gillian Hovell)

- 👁 **Lost walls** – Look ahead and around you for lines of spaced, single trees or scrubby remnants of hedging standing where a boundary once was.
- 👁 **Veteran trees** – Trees with really large gnarled trunks, especially coppiced ones with multiple trunks springing from the base, can be hundreds of years old.
- 👁 **Rocks** – Look closely at any boulders you pass: do any of them display carved markings?
- 👁 **Under your feet** – If there's something 'odd' or different on the path, stoop to take a closer look: it might be slag, charcoal, a worked flint, burnt stones or a bit of broken pottery. Take your time: an archaeological site can put up with, and indeed invites, any amount of standing and staring. Allow time to 'get your eye in' to a new site.

The beauty of archaeology is that you can look out for it at anytime – from the car or train window, as you walk down a public footpath, or as you fly over it in a plane. All you need in order to visit sites more closely is some stout footwear and appropriate protection from the elements. But better still, do a spot of homework before you go out: get a large scale OS map and pore over it looking for italicised words like *rems* (remains), *ruin*, *standing stone* or *fort*. Take the OS leisure map for Dartmoor, for example, kit yourself out with a pair of stout boots, provisions and all-weather gear and you can tramp across an ancient landscape, from prehistoric site to prehistoric

TOP TIP

When you're out and about near buildings:

Look up	Is there a date inscribed above the door?
	Is the slope of the roof exceedingly steep? Such roofs are often old and may have been thatched originally.
	Are there changes in roof line? For example, is there an old steep roof with a newer gentler sloping extension added on?
	Is there a 'scar' where a roof line once was?
	Do chimneys or windows have any noticeable styles or were they added at different dates to each other and have differing styles as a result?
Look down	Are there older, wider foundation stones at the base of the thinner walls of a newer building?
Look around	Are there larger quoin (corner) stones in the middle of a wall? The wall on the side of their 'straight' edge will be a newer extension.

site, soaking in the history as well as the rugged atmosphere and the beauty of the scenery.

If you have access to any aerial photographs whatsoever, look at them closely (using a magnifying glass helps). Countless sites have been discovered on aerial photos – indeed, Doonhill's Anglian chief's timber hall, south of Dunbar, was first spotted on aerial photos. You can ask to look at aerial photos at your local council heritage office but any aerial shot will do (Google Maps is a good internet source). You may find strange patterns of crop marks in fields, the alternating line of old ridge and furrow ploughing or unusual (and therefore probably old) field shapes.

All photographs, aerial or otherwise, are snapshots of a moment in the past: compare them with a modern OS map and you might see boundaries that are now long gone, buildings and woodlands that aren't there any more, old tracks and you may even notice the absence of modern roads. 'Map regression' is when you work backwards from modern maps to old maps and back further to even older maps. Find them on www.old-maps.co.uk and then, keeping to public access or permitted areas only, get out there and see if you can spot those altered features on the ground.

To find out what local features are already recorded you can check the national archaeological databases (the National Monument Records/Sites & Monuments Records) in the Local Council Historic Environment Records (HER) Office (many can be searched online). Check out local museums too and the Record Offices and don't forget the easily accessible books in libraries' Local History sections.

History is all around us. It speaks to us in barely heard whispers but the past is separated from us by time alone. If we know where to look, we can find it.

PART TWO

The Seven Ages of British Archaeology

THE ESSENTIALS

Britain's archaeology stretches into every corner of the land and it covers thousands of years of history. That amount of mileage in space and time can seem a daunting prospect but, just as we all split large jobs into smaller, more manageable ones, so historians split the feast that is our history into bite-sized, tastier chunks. We start with our prehistory which was monumental in its span of thousands of years as well as in the size of the henges and megaliths it left behind.

It was a Danish museum curator, C.J. Thomsen, who in 1836 divided our earliest prehistory into the Three Ages: the Stone Age (dominated by the ultimate tool box, the flint nodule), followed by the Bronze Age (when metalworking coincided with social changes) and then the Iron Age (which, historically speaking, ended with the Romans but, strictly speaking, we have never really left – we are still dependent on hard metal in every aspect of our lives, from the kitchen sink to space rockets and lifesaving medical equipment).

Since the Stone Age extends from the first stone tools ever used, c.2.5 million years ago until the Bronze Age which began in Britain a mere 2500 years ago, historians split this up too, into three smaller, more manageable pieces: the Palaeolithic (also known as the Old Stone Age – the pebble bashers), the Mesolithic (Middle Stone Age – tiny flint blades) and the Neolithic (New Stone Age – the farmers). 'Lithic' simply means 'stone-related'. Obviously these long-lived eras didn't switch from one to the other overnight; there was much overlap in culture between the boundaries of these ages.

The crucial (approximate) dates for these British prehistoric times are set out below and are shown by 'mya' (millions of years ago) and 'ya' (years ago) in the Palaeolithic.

TOP TIP

You may find these distant dates sometimes referred to as BP ('Before Present') – it means the same as 'ya' ('years ago').

TIMELINE

4 mya		Early evolution of mankind in Africa
2.5 mya		First tools – stone flakes and pebble stones. Still in Africa
700,000 ya	**Palaeolithic**	Early humans appear in Britain: Happisburgh flints and butchered bones
500,000 ya		Homo Heidelbergensis Boxgrove butchery site – flints and teardrop hand axes
450/400,000 ya		Clacton spear
300,000 ya		Swanscombe butchery sites – human skull, flint hand-axes and animal bones
230,000 ya		Homo Heidelbergensis in Wales: Pontnewydd Cave
200,000 ya		Direct DNA ancestors of all modern humans still in Africa
50,000 ya		Neanderthals in Cresswell Crags
26,000 ya		Paviland 'Red Lady' Burial (early modern man, once called 'Cro Magnon')
25,000–12,600 ya	**Ice Ages**	
15,000–13,000 ya		Cresswell Crags – earliest Palaeolithc cave art

From this point, when modern humans appear in Britain, historians use BC ('before Christ', counting backwards from Christ's birth just over 2000 years ago).

TOP TIP

You may see other initials and abbreviations used with dates:

BCE = *'Before Common Era'*. The 'Common Era' refers to dates generally referred to as AD (*anno domini* – 'in the year of the Lord'). BCE is therefore exactly the same as BC but without any reference to Christ. In other words, this does still count from Christ's birth even though it pretends it doesn't.

12,500 ya or 10500 BC	**Mesolithic**	Microlithic flint tools
10,600–8800 BC	**Warmer**	Cresswell Crags – horse head carved on bone
8800-8000 BC	**Lesser Ice Age**	
8500 BC		Humans settling in Scotland – Cramond hunting camp
7500 BC		Star Carr seasonal hunting camp
7000 BC		Gough's Cave, defleshed human bones
6000 BC		Sea levels rise and cut Britain off from mainland Europe
4000 BC	**Neolithic**	Farming begins: field systems, domesticated animals
		Cursus and long mounds.
		Portal dolmens, passage graves
3800 BC		Sweet Track
3500 BC		Early ramparts
3000 BC		Stone megalithic monuments: henges and most Neolithic
		circles

Scottish cairn rings, Irish Wedge tombs, cist burials and stone circles

2500–700 BC	**Bronze Age**	Round burial mounds with bronze grave goods and
		roundhouses
700–45 BC	**Iron Age**	Roundhouses, iron working

When the Romans arrived, they brought writing with them and so ended the 'prehistoric' (i.e. the pre-written history or records) era. The Roman occupation of Britain lasted until their departure in around AD 410 (where AD stands for *anno domini*, 'in the year of the Lord', *i.e.* counting forwards from Christ's birth).

Mesolithic hunter. (© Archaeolink Prehistory Park)

Skara Brae. (© Andrew Hovell)

Reconstruction roundhouse. (© Archaeolink Prehistory Park)

Roman Officer. (© Ermine Street Guard) Viking kit. (© Alan Ball, Vikings! Of Middle England)

55 BC–AD 410	**Roman Occupation of Britain**
55 BC	Julius Caesar invades Britain
AD 43	Emperor Claudius invades Britain
AD 410	Romans leave Britain
AD 410–1066	**Dark Ages**
563	St Columba brings Christianity from Ireland to Scotland (founds Iona monastery)
793	Vikings begin raiding, starting with Lindisfarne
1014	Danish King Cnut (Canute) takes control

When William the Conqueror invaded in 1066, a new way of life took hold in Britain and these medieval ages lasted through to about 1500. After that, this book considers history to be post-medieval, leading into the industrial and modern age: purely for simplification, the archaeology of this last era has been examined as a whole, up to the Second World War.

1066 – c.1500	**Medieval**
1066	Norman Invasion
1215	Magna Carta signed by King John
1314	Edward II defeated by Robert the Bruce at Battle of Bannockburn
1348	Black Death strikes for the first time
1415	Henry V victorious against French at Agincourt
1452	Wars of the Roses
1492	Christopher Columbus lands in America
	Post-medieval, Industrial and Modern Age
1513	English defeat Scots at Battle of Flodden
1588	Spanish Armada
1603	English and Scottish thrones unite under King James
1642	English Civil War begins

Fair Isles medieval
re-enactment group in
costume. (© Heidi Dennis, Fair
Isles Medieval Society)

The Iron bridge at Ironbridge
Gorge. (© Andrew Hovell)

1649	King Charles I beheaded
1666	Fire of London
1707	Union of English and Scottish Parliaments
1749	Hargreaves introduces Spinning Jenny
1804	Napoleon crowns himself Emperor of France
1815	British victory at Waterloo
1825	George Stephenson's Stockton to Darlington steam railway opens
1914-18	The First World War
1926	The General Strike
1939-45	The Second World War

THE STONE AGE

INTRODUCTION

The true beginning of our archaeological trail begins in Africa and goes back to around 4 million years ago, to the very dawn of mankind when the first hints of human evolution appeared and primates began to stand upright and walk on two legs. This is where archaeology is at its most vital, for without the clues dug from the ground we would know nothing of those earliest beginnings: a skull here, a few petrified footprints there … it takes all the science and skills of archaeologists to date and identify the fragmentary clues. It is not until around 2.5 million years ago that we find the first tools, fashioned from stone flakes and rounded pebbles – and at first these too were limited to Africa. These basic tools mark the start of the longest stretch of our history, our 'Stone Age'. It was to last well over 2 million years.

In Britain though, the story starts relatively late. The earliest archaeological traces of our ancestors date from about 700,000 years ago with very definite signs of human activity in the Happisburgh flint tools and butchered bones which were found as recently as 2004 in the eroding coastal cliffs of North Norfolk. But there's a snag in this: biologically Modern Man (*homo sapiens*) had not yet evolved. So who was making these tools? And, likewise, who was butchering animals 500,000 years ago using numerous teardrop-shaped hand axes and flints found in a gravel pit in Boxgrove in Sussex?

Amongst those stone tools at Boxgrove were some valuable clues: two human teeth and a thick-walled but animal-gnawed leg bone of a robust 6ft tall man who would have weighed about 80kg (12.5 stone). Our butcher, it seems was a Heidelberg Man (*homo heidelbergensis*), possibly an early ancestor of Neanderthal Man. He may not have been modern man, but he was no less human for all that – it was one of his kind who made a spearhead (found in Clacton-on-Sea in 1911) from yew wood with a skill that firmly reinforces their human status. That spear was made 100,000 years later than Boxgrove man – this was clearly a successful species. At Swanscombe in Kent, three pieces of a *homo heidelbergensis* woman's skull, from another 100,000 years on, were also found with flint hand-axes and animal remains – but still no *homo sapiens* were in sight.

Archaeological finds from this distant past are very few and far between, and the archaeological record in Britain then jumps another 70,000 years to a single tooth of yet another Heidelberg Man. Found in Pontnewydd Cave in North Wales and dating to 230,000 years ago, this tiny find is the earliest evidence we have of humans living in Wales.

Despite all this activity in Britain, it turns out that these early humans are not our direct ancestors. The relatively modern science of DNA analysis has revealed that all modern human beings are closely related to some other early humans who were still in Africa a mere 200,000 years ago. So these early finds scattered around our islands come from a different branch of humans who must have died out. As luck would have it, the archaeological record in Britain stutters during this crucial evolutionary time: for within 20,000 years of that Welsh cave dweller losing a tooth, the ice ages would descend and prevent any kind of human from living here until the glaciers retreated 120,000 years later.

Then, about 60,000 years ago, humans returned to Britain. Finds discovered in a quarry in 2002 tell us that it was not the ancient Heidelbergs who came back but Neanderthals – and, like the Boxgrove Heidelberg man 440,000 years earlier, they were still butchering large animals, but this time at a site near Thetford in Norfolk. However, they are also still our cousins, not our ancestors.

In time, humans again reached Wales, and a truly crucial discovery there brings us to the early days of modern *homo sapiens*. In a cave on the Gower coast of South Wales, a burial, labelled forever as 'The Red Lady of Paviland' was to turn out to be a man who was an early modern human (once called Cro-Magnon man but now accepted as modern in all but behaviour). He died around 26,000 years ago, aged between twenty-five and thirty years old and was only slightly smaller and lighter than the Boxgrove man. But this was no loose stray bone, this was a deliberate burial, found almost complete and stained with red ochre – ritualistic symbolism is one of the hallmarks of humanity. But other traces of human activity at this time are slight because the Ice Ages soon returned with a vengeance and humans again abandoned Britain.

When mankind returned 12,500 years later, life had moved on. It was now full of meaning: burials were elaborate and personal adornment with jewellery was popular. In the caves of the limestone gorge of Cresswell Crags in Derbyshire, a beautiful 12,000 year-old carving of a horse's head was found on a bone and, in 2003, engravings of a similar age were found on a cave wall here: a crane, a swan and a bird of prey amongst others are the oldest cave art in Britain and are only a few thousand years younger than the famous Lascaux cave paintings in France. Such works are stunning proof that the new humans in Britain were radically different from anyone who had been here before – art and the ability to conceive abstract ideas that goes with it, was part of humanity's uniqueness now – *homo sapiens* had arrived.

The warm weather lasted no more than 2000 years, and the insidious glaciers once again advanced for a last freeze across northern Britain and forced humans south once more until, just 10,500 years ago, the ice finally left for good and people could spread north again. This bout of global warming meant that modern humans, with their new 'microliths' (tiny flint blades set into tools) and their hunter-gathering Mesolithic's (Middle Stone Age) nomadic way of life were here to stay – and they reached as far west as Kendrick's Cave on Llandudno's Great Orme in around 10000 BC and as far north as Cramond near Edinburgh and on up to the Scottish islands of Orkney and Rum.

Archaeologists and historians mark this momentous change in life in Britain by classifying dates from this time on as BC. This reflects the move from intermittent prehistoric occupation to a continuity which has lasted to the present day. The retreat of the ice 10,500 years ago thus becomes 8500 BC. It was at this time that a 1.7m (5ft 6in) man with size 11 feet walked along the Severn estuary and left footprints that tell us, through the science of archaeology, that he walked at 2.6 mph and carried a heavy load on his right shoulder – had he been hunting the red deer who also left footprints here?

As the world warmed up, the melting ice caps caused the sea level to rise. In around 6000 BC Britain was cut off from the continent but this didn't stop new ideas from spreading to our islands: in about 4000 BC, a revolution that had been sweeping across the globe finally reached Britain. Domesticated cattle and sheep, together with new grain seed enabled the first farming communities in Britain. Life began to settle down and permanent monuments made of huge stones (megaliths) began to appear on the landscape. This was the Neolithic (New Stone Age), complete with community, social patterns and religion.

By 2500 BC, the first (and by far the longest) chapter in Britain's history was ending as a new material, a metal, entered the scene. A brave new Bronze Age world was dawning

◉ LOOK OUT FOR . . .

The Stone Age is, for convenience, split into the Palaeolithic (Old Stone Age) when rough stone tools were used, the Mesolithic (Middle Stone Age) with its tiny flint microlithic tools and the Neolithic (New Stone Age) when the farmers arrived. The Palaeolithic has produced little for archaeologists to find – just a few basic stone tools and bones. But such finds are extremely rare, require specialist identification and usually occur through serendipitous chance. We can, however, visit various caves which our early Palaeolithic ancestors lived in. If you walk by the Welsh caves at Pontnewydd and Paviland's Goats Cave or the high arch-like Thor's Cave near Wetton in Staffordshire there is little else to see except the view – of course, you can still gaze within and join the imaginative school of archaeology and wonder just what happened here all those millennia ago.

Tours in places like Cresswell Crags in the Cheddar Gorge help us to experience a greater sense of what Neanderthal and Mesolithic cave life may have been all about but some Mesolithic rock shelters have an extra, hidden clue – look out for grassy mounds of discarded shells (middens) outside these rough rock dwellings. Some shelters, like the one at Sand on the Applecross peninsular in Scotland also have signboards to help us to use our imagination as we hunker down beneath the rocks or share a view which must be little changed from the one those hunter-gatherers looked at. In the end though, it is impossible to detect which caves have been used and lived in simply by looking at them – 'seeing' the history here depends on being given facts about excavated finds.

And so we move on to features we *can* see for ourselves around us today. When farming arrived in Britain, communities had to settle down to manage their crops. They became settled enough to build monuments and by the end of the Neolithic the land was filled with grand earthwork and stone structures, much as churches are

The Mesolithic rock shelter at Redpoint.
(© Liz Forrest)

scattered across the landscape today. We can recognise these Neolithic monuments by looking out for certain features.

Of course, over 6000 years, they have all been worn down by natural erosion, flattened by ploughing or smothered and smashed by later building. Those that survived did so because generation after generation have respected the site, or because the stones were just too big to be moved or too darned far from settlements to be worth scavenging the stones from. So what is left for us to see?

- 👁 **Causewayed enclosures** are large, distinctive and very early features which are found mostly in southern and midland England with some occurring in the north. They're tricky to find; even the famous triple circuits of Windmill Hill at Avebury has almost been eroded out. But look for a very large flat area surrounded by a circular ditch (once 3–4m wide and 2m deep) which has multiple entrances (causeways) across it, so that the ditch is divided into numerous sections. The soil from the series of ditches will be piled up into a bank (broken only by the various entrances into the central area) which runs around the inside of the ditch. Archaeologists interpret them as trading/meeting places with some ceremonial use due to the remains of feasting and dislocated human bones within the ditches. They seem to have fallen from use by around 2500 BC but signs of settlements, such as at Crickley Hill in Gloucestershire and Carn Brea in Cornwall, have also been found within them and Iron Age forts were later built on the same sites (as at Hembury in Devon and Hambledon Hill in Dorset).

- 👁 **Cursus monuments** can be found throughout mainland Britain. They were long narrow earthwork structures and are among the earliest Neolithic monumental buildings. Edged by a bank of earth with an outer ditch, the rectangular area inside may have contained posts and some have a mound along their centre (like Cleaven Dyke's 1.8km-long mound in Perthshire) but most are now little more than dents in the ground and we can see them most clearly in crop marks on aerial photographs. Their sheer scale identifies them: the biggest, Cranborne Chase Cursus in Dorset is over 10km long and 100m wide. With little dating evidence surfacing from them, they remain enigmatic sites but they may be ritualistic processional routes or sporting sites and are often linked to other Neolithic monuments – Thornborough Henges in North Yorkshire were built on top of a cursus, and the Dorset Cursus and Stonehenge's cursus are linked to nearby long barrows.

◉ **Long barrows** began to appear soon after 4000 BC – long, rectangular mounds of earth, recognisable by a grand entrance at the wider end, leading into a small covered stone passage and a burial chamber of various designs. Much of the mound is just earth piled over the chamber and passage. They seem to have been in fashion for over 500 years and range from 25m to 120m long and survive in various states of collapse. Most archaeological evidence about Neolithic communities comes from these remarkably numerous communal burial sites and there are many we can explore internally to familiarise ourselves with their range of features: Wiltshire is particularly rich in long barrows, and take a torch to crawl into barrows like Hetty Pegler's Tump (Uley Long Barrow) in Gloucestershire. Many, like Lanyon Quoit in Cornwall, have long since lost their earthen mound.

◉ **Passage graves** took over from long barrows which became obsolete and were blocked off. Neat round mounds cover a stone passage leading into one or more central chambers with slabbed or beautifully corbelled roofs. They range from the massive La Hougue Bie on Jersey to the more usual Bryn Celli Ddu and Barclodiad y Gawres on Anglesey (which have the bonus of rare Neolithic art etched into their stones). Irish passage graves began quite small (Moneydig in Derry is dinky; a bigger version is Craigs Lower in Co. Antrim) but over the centuries bigger and more impressive mounds were built, culminating in Dowth, Knowth and Newgrange in southern Ireland's magnificent Boyne Valley complex.

◉ **Portal tombs** (also known as dolmens) occur in numbers across Wales and West England as well as Ireland. These monuments really do feel ancient – bodies were laid between the rough, solid upright stones which prop up tilting capstones that look as heavy as they are. Whether they were covered with earth is uncertain.

Bryn Celli Ddu. (© Gillian Hovell)

- **Wedge tombs** are only found in Ireland and were the last megalithic tombs to appear there in the Neolithic age. They range from simple boxes of stone slabs with a large boulder capstone, to longer galleries which may have a chamber at the end, but all the tombs slope downward to their narrower back end (hence the 'wedge' name) and they originally contained cremated remains. Although they are most common in the southwest region of Ireland, Loughash in Tyrone is a fine example and Ballygroll's prehistoric complex in Londonderry includes a wedge tomb from the end of the Neolithic as well as a court tomb and later Bronze Age circles, barrow and cairn.

- **Court cairns or chambered court tombs** are limited to southwest Scotland (mainly in Argyll and Dumfries and Galloway) and to central and northern Ireland where they seem to have originated. Also called horned cairns, they vary in style but are remarkable for their concave stone-lined courtyards which lead directly into long galleries lined with smaller cells, all of which have then been covered by a cairn edged by kerbstones.

- **Henges** are large, roughly circular or oval earthworks that originated in the late Neolithic period. Edged by a ditch with an outer bank (the opposite to cursus boundaries) they had anything between one or four entrances cutting through the bank. Built for purposes which remain unknown, it seems that inside that arena just about anything was acceptable: stone circles or rows, postholes, standing stones or burials (Bryn Celli Ddu's burial mound in Anglesey was built around 2700 BC on top of an earlier henge monument just as Ballynahatty in Co. Down has a passage tomb in the centre of Ireland's largest earthwork henge – it's an impressive 190m across).

  Henge sizes range from Wiltshire's Durrington Walls' 20m diameter (its tall banks can still be seen) to Avebury's massive 200m span. Multiple henges also exist – Thornborough Henges in North Yorkshire consists of not just one but three huge henges.

- **Megalithic** (that is, 'huge-stoned') monuments are the classic marker of Neolithic activity. Stone circles vary in diameter and in number and size of stones and are a uniquely British monument, occurring nowhere else in Europe (where alignments or single stones were preferred). For atmospheric location, you can't beat Castlerigg Stone Circle near Keswick in the Lake District, but circles can range from the Stonehenge's sarsen stones (each weighing 40 tonnes) and the towering slabs of Orkney's Stones of Stenness and the Ring of Brodgar to the dumpy Merry Maidens in Cornwall.

- **Standing stones** were also put up in avenues and linear patterns, such as the Callanish standing stones on the Scottish island of Lewis, which radiate out into a cross shape from a central stone circle surrounding a single 4.8m-tall pillar. The pale weathered stones erected at this site 5000 years ago have a harsh beauty all of their own (*colour plate 4*).

- **Neolithic houses** were often timbered wattle and daub structures with thatched roofs, so we don't find their remains easily, but where timber was in short supply, stones were used instead and we are fortunate that some of the best preserved prehistoric settlements in Europe are in Britain. Orkney's Knap o'Howar and Skara Brae are stunning examples.
- **Stony grass mounds** piled up outside Neolithic houses may be 'burnt mounds' of reddened, friable stones. Ancient water-boilers, these seem to have been heated in fires and then dropped in water to heat it before being discarded as they cooled (*colour plate 5*).
- **Neolithic monuments** were often built in association with each other – monumental complexes frequently occur across Britain: Avebury is full of monuments from every part of the Neolithic's 2000-year history, while Scotland's Kilmartin Valley contains a wonderful variety of prehistory monuments including five chambered cairns, and Machrie Moor is a Neolithic landscape of chambered cairns, stone circles, alignments and even henges.

Scan the surface of places where the sand and soil have been eroded or churned up. This causes finds that have been buried for millennia to be exposed on the surface – public beaches and the edges of public footpaths across ploughed fields are hotspots. Look out for worked flints or hand axes chipped into shape. Ideally use a GPS (or mark an OS map) to record where they were found *before* you leave the exact spot – you'd be amazed at how utterly impossible it is to remember later exactly which grassy lump or boulder you were near!

TOP TIP

Take your find to the local Finds Liaison Officers of the Portable Antiquities Scheme (their locations are on www.finds.org.uk). This way you get the best experts to identify what you've got and the site and description of your find can be recorded as part of the bigger archaeological picture.

Where to Go

There is a remarkably diverse range of excellent Stone Age sites to visit although the best are inevitably the more substantial remains from the Neolithic rather than the earlier Palaeolithic and Mesolithic. Don't fail to buy the guidebooks from the sites and read the signboards to get a real sense of history in these amazing places.

Map of Britain: Stone Age sites.
(© Andrew Hovell)

Grimes Graves, Norfolk

1 Grimes Graves in Norfolk is a truly unique site: it's the only Neolithic flint mine in Britain which is open to visitors. An almost lunar landscape of over 400 grassy craters greets you but the real attraction is 9m below ground. Around 5000 years ago, prized quality flint was mined here using simple red-deer antler picks and you can climb down a ladder to the bottom of one of the shafts and peer into the galleries that radiate out in all directions. It's dark, cramped and a hard hat is a must, but it's also unforgettable.

Orkney

2 Orkney is a must-see place for Neolithic remains. Skara Brae (which was inhabited from 3100 to 2500 BC) on the Orkney mainland is unforgettable. Like at Knap o'Howar on Orkney's tiny island of Papa Westray (two stone-built houses dating back to 3600–3100 BC), the locals used stone in the absence of timber on these bare, windswept shores. Visit both and notice how the stone hearths, beds, shelves and cupboards are strikingly similar.

Pentre Ifan, Pembrokeshire

3 Portal tombs (dolmens) are awesome and there are so many to choose from. Pentre Ifan (built c.3500 BC) in Pembrokeshire is one of the most visually dramatic in Britain (*colour plate 6*). Carreg Samson, also in Pembrokeshire (and on this book's cover), has a stunning view too and its massive capstone is supported 2m above the ground. Co. Tyrone, like all of Ireland, is rich in prehistoric monuments: Athenree has a partially collapsed capstone but its size still impresses.

Anglesey

4 Barclodiad y Gawres and Bryn Celli Ddu on Anglesey offer a chance to see rare Neolithic art as well as to explore chambered tombs. You can get into Barclodiad y Gawres by going to the shop down the road and being accompanied by a guide – precautions sadly prompted recently by vandals adding graffiti to the stones – but the swirls, lozenges and zigzags are worth it. Bryn Celli Ddu has a standing stone (a replica for similar reasons) with enigmatic zigzags on – and you can shuffle into the chamber and feel the millennia close in around you.

Maes Howe, Orkney

5 The greatest passage tomb has to be Maes Howe in Orkney. It dominates the landscape, has a soaring and beautiful corbelled vault rising 3.8m above you and passing from the megalithic passageway into the chamber is something you will never forget. Viking runic inscribed graffiti in this monumental home for the dead adds an extra dimension. In contrast, if you want to scare yourself, wriggle into Barpa Langass' chambered cairn on North Uist.

Bryn Celli Ddu on Anglesey has rare Neolithic art on the pillar. The burial mound you can crawl into was built as the Neolithic Age passed away (© Gillian Hovell)

TOP TIP

A 'corbelled' roof is one where the roof is made up of courses or layers of stones, each one projecting further inwards that the one below until they meet at the top. There is something quite breathtaking about them.

The Ring of Brodgar on Orkney.
(© Liz Forrest)

Ring of Brodgar, Orkney

6

For stone circles, it's yet again Orkney that scores in the 'Don't miss' category. Combine your trip to Maes Howe with a visit to the dramatic Ring of Brodgar and gaze in awe at the Stones of Stenness.

Isbister's Tomb of Eagles, Orkney

7

Still on Orkney, Isbister's Tomb of the Eagles is like a hybrid tomb, a stalled cairn with side chambers, built c.3000 BC (*colour plate 7*). As you crawl or drag yourself on the super little trolley provided along the low entrance passage, you enter an enclosed world. This communal tomb held dislocated bones and was a crucial piece in the Neolithic archaeological jigsaw. Intriguingly, it also housed sea eagles' bones, presumed relics of the tribe's symbolic 'totem' identity and the reason it is now so romantically named. The land owner excavated it himself and his small museum is personal and fascinating – you even get to handle stuff if you ask nicely. For an English chambered barrow, Wayland's Smithy in Oxfordshire is a great example.

Avebury

8

Avebury has virtually every Neolithic monument you could hope to see and every one is built to impress. This World Heritage Site contains the henge (with a ditch that was originally a startling 10m deep) which encloses the largest stone circle in Europe (427m across) containing nearly one hundred 40-tonne stones. Kennet Long Barrow with its sarsen entrance stones, forecourt and two burial chambers stretches away from it for 104m, and dates from 3700 BC, as does the once great but now worn down gathering place of the causewayed enclosure at Windmill Hill. West Kennet Avenue later joined Avebury to the Neolithic stone circle 2km away called The Sanctuary, and another avenue links it to the ruined Beckhampton Cove. Neolithic Silbury Hill is nearby: the tallest man-made mound in Europe (nearly 40m high), its base is a perfect circle of 167m across and yet its purpose remains a mystery.

The Dorset Cursus

9

Cursus are difficult to spot but if you walk north along Ackling Dyke to Oakley Down Barrow you can make out the line of the Dorset Cursus in the fields to the east.

10 Loughash, Co. Tyrone and Ballygroll, Londonderry

Although wedge tombs are most common in the southwest region of Ireland, Loughash in Co. Tyrone is a fine example and Ballygroll's prehistoric complex in Londonderry includes a wedge tomb from the end of the Neolithic as well as a court tomb and later Bronze Age circles, barrow and cairn.

11 Grey Cairns, Camster

Annaghmore and Clontygora Court cairns in South Armagh have excellent forecourts bounded by huge orthostats. But an unmissable example is the Long Cairn of the Grey Cairns of Camster in the Highlands. Their remoteness had undoubtedly helped to preserve them and you'll need a torch as you shuffle down the passage. The Long Cairn is 60m long and is really two round cairns joined together creating a humped feature with a horned forecourt at either end. Make sure you visit the nearby Round Cairn (a passage grave) as it boasts a fine megalithic chamber with an almost complete corbelled roof.

12 The Boyne Valley

Neolithic ritual sites often include several overlapping or connected features and, even though it's in Southern Ireland, we have to mention the Boyne Valley – it's simply one of the best. Brú na Bóinne (the Bend of the Boyne) is a busy place; a settlement dating right back to the start of the farming revolution in around 4000 BC lies close to nearly forty passage tombs built between 3200 and 2900 BC and a series of embanked earthwork enclosures, a cursus, several post rings and a stone circle. On the same ridge, three fantastic circular passage tomb mounds lie at the heart of this World Heritage Site: Dowth with its two chambers in the mound is surrounded by kerbstones (some decorated); Knowth's huge mound houses the greatest concentration of megalithic art in Western Europe and is surrounded by seventeen satellite tombs; and the third and greatest reconstructed passage tomb, Newgrange, is also stuffed full of engraved art.

What was life like?

The early Stone Age, the Palaeolithic, was the time of the hunters. The few remains of their life that we have in Britain consist largely of bits of human bone and butchery tools alongside the animal bones they were used on. Those human bones tell us that *homo Heidelbergensis* (such as that found at the Boxgrove site) were robust individuals, used to a strenuous life that followed the migrating herds, and analysis of the teeth gives testament to a decidedly carnivorous diet – and the animal bones nearby imply that horse, rhinoceros and red and roe deer may have been on the menu. But such prey was also dinner for bears, leopards, lion and an extinct species of wolf, and it is possible that humans may have even scavenged their kills. Experiments have shown that hammerstones were used to smash bones to extract the nutritious marrow and that flint blades were surprisingly efficient at cutting and skinning the animals. Then, around 60,000 years ago, Neanderthals roamed Britain, making tools, hunting in organised groups and burying their dead. Stocky and strong, they were the masters of the Ice Ages.

By 26,000 years ago, early humans were able to think in abstract terms and were carefully and ritually burying their clothed and jewellery-adorned (but apparently headless) dead in red ochre. Rituals serve to satisfy a spiritual dimension in life – were the unexplained spatulae and tooled mammoth ivory rods left beside the grave centuries later also part of rituals? Human life and death was now a far cry from that gnawed human leg bone found at Boxgrove.

When the final ice age retreated in around 11000 BC, warmth and plants returned to Britain, closely followed by animals such as elephants, bears, wolves, rhinos, bison, lynx and the terrifying huge ox, the aurochs – and humans followed the packs and herds along coasts and rivers, moving camp as and when to get the best from the world around them. Although Ireland developed its own larger 'Bann flakes', Mesolithic hunters on Britain's mainland used tiny but very sharp flint blades called microliths to hunt animals and birds and they even inserted these tiny blades into hafts to make harpoons for fishing: the middens at places like Oronsay off Scotland's west coast and Morton in Fife suggest that seafood was a major source of the Mesolithic diet.

At the waterlogged site of Star Carr in North Yorkshire, a Mesolithic camp on the fringes of a lake has been excavated: wild animals that had been killed for meat were cooked at hearths, hides were prepared by scraping to supply both clothing and shelter, sinews provided thread, hooves were boiled into glue, and bones were worked into tools, spearheads, needles, bead and pendants – nothing was wasted.

But were those tiny sharp blades used for something altogether more sinister? Gough's Cave in Somerset's Cheddar Gorge has thought-provoking evidence of skinning marks on human skulls and marrow-extraction from human long bones. They suggest that, in about 7000 BC, defleshing of corpses was practised here – was it cannibalism? Or was it part of the ritual that preceded the burial of the disarticulated bones of both adults and children that were found here? After all, burying loose bones was common practice which survived for at least another 3000 years.

Even in around 4000 BC, when knowledge of farming arrived in Britain, loose bones were still being buried, piled up in the long barrow tombs that were now being constructed to mark communities' precious newly managed lands. Isbister in Orkney contained a jumble of bones belonging to over 300 individuals and West Kennet contained over fifty disarticulated people. This communal mixing up (and apparent sharing out) of ancestors' relics in the Stone Age helps to show us that time was not seen as linear. Lives did not step from the past into the present and on into the future, but the present existed as a part of (not just a continuation of) the past – its identity, purpose and day-to-day meaning (not just its history) was been bound up in the stories of what had gone before. The lack of skulls and leg bones at West Kennet

Disarticulated bones were a part of life in the Neolithic. (© Tomb of the Eagles)

hints at 'relics' being shared around amongst family members – maybe the stone dressers in the Neolithic houses so well preserved at Orkney's Skara Brae displayed an ancestor's skull in pride of place? It may seem alien to us, but in many present-day ancient cultures life is still lived in the company of ancestors.

Outside the Neolithic homes, 'ritual landscapes' abounded, with causewayed enclosures, henges and cursus monuments dominating vast tracts of land: life certainly had a symbolic and spiritual dimension for the new farmers.

From around 4000 BC, farming allowed more people to live in a smaller area and so communities built up, as at Cornwall's Carn Brea hilltop settlement. Houses of the time were far from primitive – Orkney's Skara Brae homes even seem to have inside toilets. Around the houses were small field plots dotted with stone clearance cairns. The dogs who had helped to manage the Mesolithic wild herds now rounded up new breeds of domesticated cattle (the fierce native aurochs could never have been tamed). Sheep and goats were kept too, while pigs grubbed in the woodlands that remained outside the axe-slashed and burned clearances.

Chopped wood could be skilfully used for house timbers and wattle walls, dinnerware, tools and arrow shafts and complex bows – the 1.9m-long Meare Bow (c.3425 BC) is only 1.5cm thick and the equally long but narrower Ashcott bow (3400 BC) found in the Somerset Levels were both skilfully made of yew, while dugout canoes and wooden trackways gave access across the seas and over the inimitable boglands. It is little wonder that the axe which supplied the wood and transformed the land became the iconic symbol of the time, with decorative but impractical and useless axes being prized and made in abundance in axe factories like the one at the remote Pike o'Stickle in Cumbria. Much valued, these were traded over large distances.

An efficient nomadic hunting lifestyle had been the favoured way of life for 99 per cent of humanity's time on earth but, once life had settled down, heavy pottery in the form of rough, round-bottomed pots, fashioned from coils or flattened strips of clay could be made and used. From 3800 BC regional decorated styles appear and, from around 2800 BC, 'Grooved Ware' (flat-bottomed and bucket-shaped) spread from the northern isles.

Over time, burial habits changed too, and they illustrate a change in social mores: round houses replaced the rectangular homes (look for the later roundhouses at Skara Brae) and, after about 3000 BC new graves followed the pattern as rounded mounds and ring cairns took over from long barrows. Circular henges (and, later, stone circles) also began to litter the land. By 2500 BC, a dramatic shift to individual burials, sometimes accompanied by grave goods, was heralding a new era which would later be forever identified with a new metal: the Bronze Age was dawning.

Things to do

There are numerous museums where you can discover more about the various Stone Age periods. Amongst the grandest, London's Natural History Museum explores man's evolution while the British Museum displays a range of stone tools. While you're in the area, tour the Horniman Museum in London's Forest Hill – it was established on its excellent collections of British prehistoric materials, including flint tools from important sites such as Swanscombe and Grimes Graves.

Away from London, virtually every regional museum has some stone axe or flints on display. You can see a particularly good display of Palaeolithic axes and other archaeological finds at Hertford Museum, while you can handle Palaeolithic tools at Torquay Museum. If you're in the area, tour nearby Kents Cavern, a natural cave system which was home to Stone Age people between 500,000 and 12,000 years ago.

Cresswell Crags Museum and Archaeology Park (with its proposed brand new Ice Age Centre) is justly proud of its reputation as one of Britain's top heritage sites. It is home to Britain's earliest cave art (13,000 years old), recently discovered in Church Hole in 2003, including birds and a possible ibex, hatched patterns, a human figure and a horse's head. The new centre should provide an inspiring and comfortable, all facilities available, visitor and education attraction. Go to www.creswell-crags.org.uk.

Somerset's Cheddar Caves enable you to walk down into their caves and they enjoy their reputation as Britain's 'first authenticated cannibal site' as well as, telling you 'everything conventional museums won't tell you about life and death in the Stone Age'. Go to www.cheddarcaves.co.uk

Even if you can't get to a site or a national or local museum, marvel at the fine Mesolithic tiny microlithic flints or the difference between them and the Palaeolithic hand axes by checking out the images section of the Portable Antiquities Scheme's website, www.findsdatabase.org

Or you can take a virtual tour of several Neolithic henges and stone circles on Chris Collyer's wonderful website, www.stone-circles.org.uk. 360° panoramas give you stunning views which make you feel as if you're really standing in the centre of fantastic sites such as Castlerigg's stone circle and 'Long Meg and Her Daughters'.

A reconstruction Mesolithic camp is just one of the scenes on offer at the Archaeolink Prehistory Park. (Reproduced with permission from Archaeolink Prehistory Park)

If you want a more hands-on approach, put 'flint knapping' into an internet search engine and pick a workshop or course where you can learn this ancient art. Be warned: it's not as simple as you might think – there was nothing 'primitive' about these tools. And if just a few flint artefacts aren't enough to help you to imagine life in the Mesolithic, take a trip to Aberdeenshire and tour the Archaeolink Prehistory Park. A reconstructed hunter-gatherer camp with a shell-midden and a dug-out canoe, together with leather-drying and meat-smoking racks will make the flint-knappers feel more human. This multi-award winning living history park will enable you to sample any prehistoric era, right up to the Romans, and it has a packed programme of events too. Check it out www.archaeolink.co.uk

Reading up

There is plenty of archaeological debate to make up for the scarcity of hard evidence out there. A fascinating read into our prehistoric beginnings is Colin Renfrew's thought-provoking *Prehistory: Making of the Human Mind* (W&N 2007). *Prehistoric Britain* by Prof. Timothy C. Darvill (Routledge 1998) outlines the earliest history of our islands, while the broader picture from 700,000 years ago is given in detail in *Prehistoric Europe*, edited by Barry Cunliffe (Oxford University Press 1994). *Homo Britannicus: The Incredible Story of Human Life in Britain* by Chris Stringer, director of the Ancient Human Occupation of Britain Project (AHOB), analyses the rare prehistoric finds of mankind in Britain from an authoritative viewpoint, but those of a nervous disposition should be warned that it includes a final terrifying word about the impact global warming can have on the world.

Narrowing in on each era, the Palaeolithic is considered in Nicholas Barton's well-illustrated *Stone Age Britain* (Batsford/English Heritage 1997) and Erek Roe's *The Lower and Middle Palaeolithic Periods in Britain* (Routledge 1981).

The Mesolithic is covered by a number of very different books: *Mesolithic Britain* by John Wymer (Shire Archaeology 1991) is a short summary while *Late Stone Age Hunters of the British Isles* by Christopher Smith (Routledge 1992) is more detailed, and Graeme Warren's *Mesolithic Lives in Scotland* (Tempus Publishing 2005) gives a good sense of the time and the place. The Batsford/Historic Scotland series includes *Scotland's First Settlers* by Caroline Wickham-Jones (1994).

Specific books on the Neolithic include the good short introduction, *Neolithic Britain* by Joshua Pollard (Shire Archaeology 1997) and Julian Thomas' *Understanding the Neolithic* (Routledge, 1999). Francis Pryor's *Farmers in Prehistoric Britain* (Tempus 1998) explores the Neolithic onwards.

Stone Age sites in particular are explored in a number of books. Just two of them are *Fairweather Eden* by Michael Pitts and Mark Roberts (Century 1977) which describes over ten years of excavations at Boxgrove, including the discovery of the 500,000 year-old Boxgrove Man, and *Star Carr Revisited* by A.J. Legge and P.A. Rowley-Conwy (University College London 1988) which takes a look back at the work on this important Mesolithic site. *Prehistoric Orkney* by Anna Ritchie (Historic Scotland/Batsford Ltd 1995) takes you round the islands' archaeological riches, and *Neolithic and Bronze Age Scotland* by P.J. Ashmore (Historic Scotland/Trafalgar Square Publishing 1997) is a clear and enjoyable read.

Bob Bewley concentrates on *Prehistoric Settlements* (Batsford/English Heritage 1994) but *Prehistoric Britain from the Air* by Timothy Darvill (Cambridge University Press 1996) gives us a bird's eye view of the sites.

To dig deeper into the Stone Age, log on: *ww.nhm.ac.uk/hosted_sites/ahob/index_2. html* to follow the fascinating high profile AHOB (Ancient Human Occupation of Britain) Project.

THE BRONZE AGE

INTRODUCTION

The next one and a half millennia would be classified by historians as the Bronze Age, a time of change when mankind moved from the millennia of the Stone Age into the dawning of modern civilisation. For changes were afoot: not only were the first metalworking skills crossing the channel in c.2500 BC, but there were some dramatic social changes occurring at home. While the uniquely British henges and megaliths continued, roundhouses were coming to dominate the domestic scene. In death, individuals were now being buried in their own private, smaller, round and, more importantly, sealed up mounds – there was no intention of unearthing and sharing out these bones like their ancestors had done. No longer were family and community identity enough: personal status in the here-and-now was what mattered. A culture of honoured individuals (such as Boscombe Down's 'Avebury Archer') was growing. The dead were buried with their prized possessions, including the new smart metal daggers: perhaps you really could 'take it with you'. Modern materialism had arrived.

But change was slow. Even as the so-called Beaker people swept across Britain between 2300-2000 BC bringing handleless tall beakers with them, the enduring flint arrowheads were still buried in graves alongside the bronze, copper and gold grave goods. In a similar fashion, the old fashioned stone battle axes continued to be laid alongside the latest beautifully and richly decorated metal daggers.

From around 1700 BC, the Wessex culture prospered, with its rich round barrow graves and the golden cups that echo the contemporary treasures found within the great Cyclopean walls of Agamemnon's Mycenae in Greece. And around this time, Stonehenge was taking its final shape, surrounded by the many round burial mounds that we can see today.

A population explosion meant more land began to be farmed and new farms gradually expanded into the less favourable corners of the land. Between around 1500 BC and 1250 BC (the Middle Bronze Age) a favourable change in the climate enabled a huge exploitation of even the remotest upland areas such as the Dartmoor uplands and Bodmin Moor. Thousands of new settlements of roundhouses encircled by boundary walls appeared and a surprising number of them can still be recognised today. Trackways linked these settlements and our modern roads sometimes still follow those ancient routes while traces of others can still be seen on aerial photos.

At this time, cremation followed by burial of the ashes in large open cemeteries became fashionable. Individuals' remains were still kept safe and isolated by placing them in a private patch in their own personal urn but the once essential grave goods were absent now. Meanwhile, Ireland adopted simplified boulder burials and stone circles such as Drombeg – all at a time when Tutankhamun was being buried in splendour in Egypt.

However, with the Late Bronze Age (c.1250–700 BC) came troubled times: the warriors no longer carried all-purpose daggers but slashing swords, designed specifically for killing other humans; and new defensive hillforts with daunting ramparts were being built. What caused this violent change?

The answer is hidden in the remains of prehistoric oaks: their starved growth rings tell of a devastating twenty years of drastic climate change, potentially caused by an almighty Icelandic volcanic eruption in around 1159 BC. The darkness and unremitting cold must have felt like the end of the world. Whole populations right across Britain were forced to head down from the now thinning upland sites and into tense competition for farmland. Horse riding was now no longer not just a wondrous new form of transport but a tool of warfare too. This society revelled in ostentatious warlike displays and feasted from brand new pottery styles – hints of what we now consider the hallmarks of the up-and-coming Celtic lifestyle. Even as bronze gave way to a new, harder metal, iron, stone circles were still being built but the margins of life, the watery depths like those at Flag Fen, had developed into a powerful spiritual recipient of valuable and sacrificial offerings. Change was in the air again.

Of course, life didn't change overnight between the prehistoric ages. New materials, styles and habits were adopted slowly, often over generations, but eventually certain fashions came out on top and the Bronze Age was no exception. Certain distinctive features identify a number of monuments as Bronze Age in date – especially the burial mounds.

👁   ***Round burial mounds*** are the most common prehistoric monuments in Britain and can be found everywhere. They vary in design, but all were earthen mounds piled over a burial or cremation. These are the burial mounds which are marked on maps as *tumulus*. Some are now little more than unnamed ploughed-out lumps or crop marks in the middle of fields but others in areas like Stonehenge and Bully Hills in Lincolnshire have several grouped together to form a cemetery.

TOP TIP

round barrows come in various shapes – see if you can spot the differences when you're out and about:

bowl barrows had a ditch and a bank around them;

bell barrows were on a level platform with a ditch around;

disc barrows were small barrows on a large platform with a ditch and bank around;

saucer barrows were low mounds ending straight into a ditch and bank;

pond barrows were circular hollows with an outer bank containing cremations, burials and even dismembered burials.

In Scotland, cairns (piles of stones), rather than earth, were heaped over a grave. Look out for those with a kerb around the edge, as at Cairnpapple Hill, west of Edinburgh. Sometimes a single cairn would cover several individual graves each laid in a stone box (cist). The Kilmartin cairns give you several fantastic examples in one self-contained valley while the Ballymeanoch cairn is a neat example of how the kerb can survive around a worn-out mound.

The Clava Cairns near Inverness are a group of three amazing late Neolithic/early Bronze Age chambered cairns nestling in a wooded glade. Here the cairns are edged by kerbstones and have a circle of standing stones around the outside. Two of the cairns each have a passage which faces the midwinter solstice and leads into a wonderful corbelled chamber which is topped with a capstone.

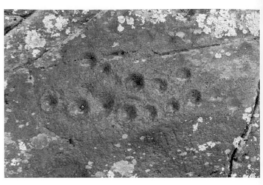

Clava Cairns. (© Liz Forrest)   Simple cup-and-ring carvings. (© Gillian Hovell)

Ireland had a different approach: wedge tombs continued from the Stone Age, the only difference now being that the cremated remains were now accompanied by beakers and maybe some bronze artefacts. The tombs of this time ranged from plain stone-slabbed boxes to galleries with a chamber at the end, but they all have the distinctive roof slab which sloped down away from the entrance.

In the later Bronze Age (c.1500-800 BC) Ireland's wedge tombs gave way to boulder burials which were little more than a pit holding charcoal and cremated bones covered by three or four upright stones supporting a large boulder as a capstone – no chamber, no cairn, no covering mound were created.

The beautiful Isles of Scilly were far enough removed to develop their own particular style of Bronze Age communal burial chambers. Although they look like normal barrows, their round or oval mound is made of tightly packed stones and soil. Porth Hellick Down's 'entrance grave' clearly demonstrates the kerb, inner passage and capped chamber. Innisidgen Upper burial cairn is also especially well preserved. They can range from 3m to over 20m in diameter.

 *Cup-and-ring carved rocks* were made throughout the Bronze Age and even for years on either side (a grand total of c.3000 years) and they are certainly stunningly enigmatic. This new and distinctive art form appears on numerous isolated earth fast boulders in North Yorkshire and Northumbria, as well as throughout Scotland where whole outcrops of rocks are sometimes smothered in a wide-range of carved cup and concentric rings (as at Galloway and Argyll's Lochgilphead). Were they 'ritual', or boundary markers, or possibly some form of map either of the locality or of the stars? Who knows?

The carvings can be subtle and difficult to spot as the millennia have sometimes eroded them into a mere echo of their original depth and sharpness. The best time to find and see them is on a winter's morning or late afternoon, when the sun is low and the shadows of the carvings are clearly picked out.

👁 **Standing stones** are often Neolithic but a number seem inextricably linked to Bronze Age burial mounds so an open mind (and a helpful signboard or a spot of site research before your visit) is required to guess their age. Similarly, rows of standing stones may have Neolithic origins but several date from the Bronze Age and a few have Bronze Age carvings on them (Ballymeanoch's row of four tall stones in Scotland includes one which is carved with no fewer than seventy Bronze Age cup marks, thirteen of which have rings around them, and a second stone here has forty cup marks and two cup and rings. The three Devil's Arrows near Boroughbridge in North Yorkshire look very different but are considered to be the dramatic remains of a Bronze Age row of standing stones.

👁 **Stone circles** continued from the Neolithic, although Bronze Age examples were often smaller in scale than the Stone Age megaliths and date from between 2000 to 1000 BC. Occurring throughout Britain, they vary from the circles of Gors Fawr in Dyfed to Appletreewick's squat stones in North Yorkshire while there are many stone circles in the south-west peninsula of Britain: seventy stone circles stand on the uplands of Dartmoor alone and another sixteen, including the Hurlers, are scattered on Bodmin Moor. Even the remote and boggy Machrie Moor on the Isle of Arran is an evocative Bronze Age site, full of stone circles, standing stones, cairns and hut circles.

The north-east of Scotland revels in recumbent stone circles. A sub-species of smallish stone circles found near hilltops, these are identified by a large prostrate stone (sometimes bearing cup marks) laid across an entrance flanked by the two tallest upright stones. The standing stones taper downwards in height away from the south-western entrance and

One of the Devil's Arrows at Boroughbridge. (© Gillian Hovell)

they may be of a different colour and type of stone from the flankers and recumbent stone. The circles appear to be aligned for lunar observations linked with the midwinter solstice. Loanhead of Daviot is a great example.

- 👁 **Enclosures** were needed to prevent livestock from wandering and traces of these walls remain in the now bleak moorland areas which were abandoned at the end of the Bronze Age. Look out for low tumbled lines of stones or surviving relics of walls with heavy orthostats (earthfast boulders) in their base – sometimes they are all that remain, sticking out of the heather like a line of broken teeth (*colour plate 8*). Don't miss the Grimspound settlement on Dartmoor where miles of ancient landscape remain untouched by later human building works.

- 👁 **Home cooking relied on fires in hearths** but, until the Late Bronze Age, there were no cauldrons which could withstand the heat and so a special feature of Bronze Age life can be found out in the fields today: boiling water involved placing stones into a regular hearth and then adding them to a nearby stone trough (or fulacht(a) fiadh(a) in Ireland) which contained the water. The hot stones heated the water and, when they cooled, they were tossed out onto a discard pile so that fresh heated stones could be added. This seems to be the origin of the piled-up crescents of reddened, burned, friable stones (called 'burnt mounds') which can be found around our islands.

- 👁 **Hillforts**. Climate change prompted land hunger, but whatever the cause, troubled times led to the concept of hillforts which certainly began in the Bronze Age – Castell Odo on the Llyn Peninsular was the earliest in Wales, dating from around 650 BC, and Mam Tor's ramparts might date from the Bronze Age huts and mounds within them (*colour plate 9*). As they multiplied and developed into the Iron Age it is difficult, in fact almost impossible sometimes, to recognise which forts belong to which age simply by walking around them – then it's down to excavation alone and the smallest of finds that lurk deep within them to date the site – so look out for signboards and read up before visiting them. Nonetheless, there is no doubt that people began building such impressive structures around 3000 years ago. Although many become disused and new ones were built elsewhere, similar forts remained a part of the living landscape for over 1000 years – that's longer than most surviving abbeys, castles and churches have graced our modern landscapes.

🚶 Where to Go

While there are a limited number of Bronze Age features to spot for ourselves 'out in the field', some of our greatest archaeological sites belong to the Bronze Age.

Map of Britain: Bronze Age sites.
(© Andrew Hovell)

Stonehenge

Of course, the most famous Bronze Age site of all is Stonehenge. Already a ritual site in the Neolithic, it was in the Bronze Age that the 2m-tall bluestone were brought 240 miles from the Preseli Hills in Wales and placed in a double horseshoe. Hundreds of years later (but still in the Bronze Age) they were moved and put inside the new sarsen stone lintelled circle and its inner horseshoe of lintelled pairs. By the end of the Bronze Age, Stonehenge looked much as its ruins do today. Look out too for the Bronze Age round barrows that are dotted around the Stonehenge landscape.

The Great Orme

The Bronze Age wouldn't be the bronze age without the copper needed to make it. To experience the sheer scale of prehistoric copper mining, don a hard hat and head underground. The Great Orme in the hillside of Llandudno in Wales was mined from around 2500 BC and burrows 6km of tunnels into the rock although a further 10km may still remain unsurveyed (*colour plate 10*). Over 1700 tonnes of copper metal (enough for 10 million axes) were extracted during the Bronze Age: copper was valuable and it was big business. It was mined using bone and stone hammer tools in tunnels lit only by animal fat candles and there is no escaping the fact that there are tunnels here which only children could have mined.

Grimspound

3   Grimspound walled settlement hauntingly tells of the upland farms that flourished in 1500 BC in this now unpopulated desolate spot of Dartmoor. A tumbled boundary wall, entered by a paved and stepped south-eastern gateway, encircles four acres. Inside are two dozen stone-walled roundhouses. Some have hearths, stone entrances and even porches angled to give protection from the elements, and others seem to have been simple animal pens. Life here flourished for 300 years but then the fields began to clog with peat as the climate changed. Well worth a visit but be prepared for the seemingly eternal mist.

Bodmin Moor

4   Another outstanding atmospheric spot is the Hurlers on Bodmin Moor. Here, three Bronze Age stone circles of different sizes stand in a row. A paved granite track linked them and, intriguingly, the central circle was paved by quartzite crystals hammered from its smoothed standing stones. The circles sit amidst a landscape almost cluttered with stone rows, standing stones, cairns and barrows – one of which had been cut into by a cist (stone box) burial in which was found a burial, complete with the spectacular Rillaton Cup (now on show in the British Museum). The whole area is simply full of rocky outcrops, later stone crosses, mines and quarries. A similar triple set of Bronze Age stone circles, linked this time by stone rows and surrounded by cairns can be found at Beaghmore in Co. Tyrone, Northern Ireland.

Flag Fen

5   Whether the settlement at Flag Fen was born out of expansion into new territories or from an attraction to a holy place is a moot point. What is clear is that, at this major archaeological site near Peterborough in Cambridgeshire, in the years just before 1000 BC tens of thousands of timbers were used to create walkways and platforms – in the waters beside the timber walkway many valuable bronze and metal goods were first broken and then 'deposited', often carefully lodged into the wood. Like at Llyn Fawr in South Wales and the River Thames, the water deities accepted these offerings.

Overton Hill

6   Although round barrows are the most common monument of the Bronze Age and can be found throughout the land, there are a few places where you can find a good collection of them. Overton Hill in Wiltshire has a cemetery of bowl and bell barrows, several of which were planted with beech trees in the eighteenth century. Take the sometimes steep South-West Coast Path at Northdown in Dorset for

a fine ridge walk among a number of barrows, or explore Lambourne Seven Barrows in Berkshire where seven barrows are grouped but nigh on twenty barrows (mostly bowl but some saucer and rare disc barrows) sit within 1km of the main cluster.

Chalk figures

7 The monumental scale of the chalk figures cut into our hillsides have traditionally be ascribed to the Bronze Age. Uffington White Horse certainly sits beneath the ancient track way called the Ridgeway and recent archaeological science has come up with a date as early as 2000 BC. However, this is the only chalk figure with any certain prehistoric pedigree. Documentary evidence rarely exists for most figures before 1700, although the Long Man of Wilmington in Sussex is associated with possible Roman fired clay fragments. Horses and men with possible spears certainly cast our minds to the warrior culture of the Bronze Age and there is some link with nearby barrows, so who knows?

Achnabreck and Kilmarton

8 While many Bronze Age monuments are on a grand scale, others are more subtle. Cup-and-ring carvings can be found on countless isolated boulders in northern England and southern Scotland but to see them in all their splendour, head up the hill at Achnabreck. A brief walk into the edge of the forest will take you to several outcrops of rocks with literally dozens of carvings. Kilmartin too is home to a great slab of rock that is smothered in carvings.

The Liddle Burnt Mound

9 The Liddle Burnt Mound is situated conveniently beside the path to the Isbister Tomb of the Eagles on Orkney. A once watertight clay-lined slabbed stone trough, measuring 1.6m x 1m and 0.6m deep, is surrounded by paving, and a peat-fuelled hearth sits nearby in a wall alcove. You can see the tell-tale pile of discarded burnt stones alongside this feature – heated in the fire they were then dropped into the water trough to boil it.

Cup-and-ring carvings at Kilmartin. (© Gillian Hovell)

The Liddle burnt mound in Orkney lies beside a flagged floor around a stone trough. (© Tomb of the Eagles)

What was life like?

When the Bronze Age began, about 4500 years ago, the climate was warmer and drier than it is today. Farmers managed to clear more and more land of the trees and they headed out onto the high ground to farm the land more intensely. They ploughed the land and then harvested the new hulled barley and the old emmer wheat with bronze sickles (and, no doubt, with flint tools too while the skills of flint-knapping continued until c.1200 BC). They dried the grain on racks and then stored it in pits and finally ground it with heavy quern stones. Cattle were herded in some considerable numbers and sheep were fully exploited for wool and meat. Goats were also kept and deer were still hunted while, over the centuries, horses gradually progressed from being food to becoming status symbols, chariot-pullers and war machines.

Even though the hardy and ever-useful flint continued to be used for centuries, bronze was the new revolutionary material in this society – it was used for stunning neckwear called torcs, sickles, jewellery and pins as well as daggers, spearheads, rapiers and leaf-shaped swords and multitudes of axe heads. As well as being useful tools, they were prized and traded great distances as things of beauty and symbolism: submerged shipwrecks have been found loaded up with vast hoards of them, probably bound for distant lands and a tidy profit. It's worth going to Dover to see the Bronze Age boat, made in around 1500 BC (and not found until 1992) which, at 18m long and 2.5m wide was rowed by at least eighteen oarsmen and undoubtedly could have crossed the Channel with a heavy cargo.

With the new prestigious metal came a new way of life, full of showy glamour. The elite dead were still buried in highly visible and carefully sited barrows on the borders of territory, but now the barrows were round instead of long, and death had become personal. Instead of the old barrows which had housed numerous dislocated and shared-out skeletons, now they usually held just one individual, buried in style, alone and shut away to ensure he or she remained intact. Sometimes they were cremated (which denied the option of relics being passed on), while grave goods were added according to status. A new priority was clearly taking hold, as the past no longer mingled with the present in the same way: individuals' lives, here and now,

Bronze Age round burial mounds sit in the shadow of Stonehenge (© Tim Darvill)

not their sacramental role as an ancestor, were what counted. Time had become linear, with lives being played out individually, one after another. These burials bear witness to this profoundly new concept of what being a human being really meant. Placed around each honoured individual were beakers, fine jewellery, valued knives and well-made weapons. The consumer society had begun and was being celebrated in death as well as in life.

TOP TIP

The richest Bronze Age Beaker burial ever found in Britain is the Amesbury Archer discovered at Boscombe Down, 3km (2 miles) from Stonehenge. He died early in the Bronze Age, sometime around 2300 BC (just as the sarsen stones were being erected at Stonehenge) and was buried with skilfully made flint arrowheads, polished stone wrist guards, decorated beakers, copper knives, gold jewellery and a black stone used for metalworking. He was definitely being buried and remembered for who he was, not as one of the hosts of ancestors.

However, these posturing individualistic barrows with their showy grave goods gradually gave way to communal graveyards filled with humble cremated ashes, the ancient sites still held sway and cremations of the Late Bronze Age have been found tucked into sites such as the Neolithic Loanhead of Daviot recumbent stone circle or lowered discreetly into the edges of earlier Bronze Age round barrows or Irish wedge tombs. This may have been due to a sense of continuing traditions, or perhaps the mourners were simply drawn to the seemingly timeless monuments in their landscape, just as we are still drawn to them today.

Valuable goods were often shared with the gods – often unused or too highly decorated for any practical use, swords and knives, shields and helmets have been found in the watery pools, lakes, rivers and bogs. But before being deposited, many offerings had been deliberately broken. Was this part of a ritual to symbolically 'kill' them as a sacrifice to the gods maybe, or was it simply to prevent the unscrupulous from retrieving such expensive items when they were intended as holy sacrifices? Our wishing wells – and the legends of King Arthur's sword Excalibur being tossed into the lake and received by the hand of the Lady of the Lake – are but pale echoes of these ancient rites.

But the good times didn't last: the weather turned against them – by 1200 BC the once fertile high ground was being smothered in widespread blanket bog. An ideal home had once been a single roundhouse surrounded by farmstead enclosures amongst a few scattered roundhouses but, as decent farmland shrivelled, land hunger grew and palisaded banks and ditches were thrown up to protect a huddled groups of huts (*e.g.* on Mam Tor in Derbyshire). Early hillforts were beginning to spread across Britain. Some were designed to impress as well as defend: ramparts constructed of compacted clay, mixed with stone and charcoal, would have been dazzling in bright sunshine and were unmistakable statements of power. The message was clear: don't mess with the inhabitants within.

And, when times were really hard, religion resorted to superstition. Remarkable burials have been found under the floors of seven roundhouses at Cladh Hallan in South Uist in the Outer Hebrides: a sheep, decapitated dog, a teenage girl, a toddler and even already ancient mummified adults had been buried beneath the house in around 1000 BC. Whatever was going on here was a very intense – we can only guess at what drove the inhabitants of the house to such extreme rituals.

Meanwhile, Irish communities gave up their fancy tombs and reverted to basic, unfussy methods of burial. Now they simply placed cremated bones in pits beneath small boxes of upright stone slabs which were uncovered except for being capped with a large boulder – these were the simple 'boulder burials' of Cork and Kerry.

Generally though, few burials of this Late Bronze Age are ever found by archaeologists. Were most ashes scattered? Were they offered to the water gods? Or where they exposed to be taken by wild animals? No one knows. But life went on, even in this new world of hardship and conflict. It seems that even the widespread trade and travel experienced at the start of the Bronze Age by the Amesbury Archer continued: the wooden Dover boat had been made in happier times (c.1500 BC) but European influences continued to be introduced even after the troubled years as overseas trends were copied and socketed bronze axes became larger as time went on.

Bronze never superseded gold as the most coveted metal – it continued to impress and *lunulae* (collars of sheet gold) were proud social statements in both Ireland and Wales. Visit the British Museum to see the stunning gold collar from Mold. But more day-to-day items included bone combs and tweezers (and maybe a bone flute or two), antler spatulae and pickaxes, horn ladles and hilts. Baltic amber pendants and beads were not uncommon and, no doubt, wooden platters, handles and tools were in daily use (although wood rarely survives for archaeologists to find). Loom weights and spindle whorls dating from the Late Bronze Age are evidence for the production of textiles although only the occasional scrap survives in a grave since most textiles have long since rotted.

Soon though, there would be another material for archaeologists to find. The art of smelting and forging iron was about to spread to the islands of Britain from its near eastern origins.

Things to do

There are relatively few major sites to visit from the Bronze Age, but they include some of the most spectacular prehistoric monuments on our islands. To understand them better, why not visit a reconstruction site or look in at a museum and prepare to be impressed as you admire the very beautiful treasures that have been unearthed from this time.

Archaeolink Prehistory Park in Aberdeenshire's award-winning park is once again the place to go: it's simply stuffed full of reconstructions which bring the Bronze Age (and other ancient ages) to life (*colour plate 11*). Bronze casting, mould and crucible making are demonstrated, as are jewellery-making and charcoal production to make fuel. You'll soon realise that this was no cultural backwater in time. See www.archaeolink.co.uk

Visit Flag Fen and you won't just see a jumble of damp preserved timbers at this important site. A recreated Bronze Age fen and village, built on a platform over the marshes is home to a timber monument of breathtaking proportions. There's treasure trove to admire here too. Pick your day carefully and you can enjoy some of the lively and imaginative events that are held here throughout the year: bards, Fenland food and weapon displays are just some of the activities on offer. See www.flagfen.org

To really grasp the beauty of the objects created in the Bronze Age, spend some time in the British Museum. It houses many of the great Bronze Age treasures: the gold Rillaton pot, the Gold Mold cape and the Ringlemere gold cup may be dented but they still look great.

The Salisbury and South Wiltshire Museum is an important centre for finds from Stonehenge which are vividly displayed in its interactive gallery. The Amesbury Archer and his grave goods are on permanent display here. See www.salisburymuseum.org.uk

The Heritage Museum in Devizes is home to one of most important Neolithic and Bronze Age collections in Britain. Go there and see more archaeological material from Stonehenge and Durrington Walls. See www.wiltshireheritage.org.uk

Chris Collyer's website www.stone-circles.org.uk includes Bronze Age stone circles (as well as Neolithic ones). Here, you can scroll down to a list of 360° panoramas – get to stand in the centre of those circles and look around! Or why not simply get out your local OS map and look for *tumuli* out in the fields. You might be surprised just how many there are.

Reading up

The Bronze Age is often included in books on prehistoric Britain generally. Francis Pryor's *Britain BC* (Harper Perennial Sep 2004) is just such a one. It's a lengthy but authoritative and readable look at prehistoric life throughout the British Isles and gives a flavour of just what life was like over two millennia ago. The early chapters of *A History of Britain: At the Edge of the World? 3000 BC–AD 1603* is Simon Schama's follow-up to his television episodes about the beginning of Britain's history (BBC Books 2000). Meanwhile, *Bronze Age Britain* by Michael Parker Pearson (English Heritage/Batsford Ltd 2005) is more specifically age-related and follows the story from the start of stone-using farmers to the end of the Bronze Age.

Plan your exploration of Bronze Age Britain with the Ordnance Survey's *Ancient Britain* historical map (2005) – sites of interest in every corner of our islands are flagged up.

The Megalithic Portal (www.megalithic.co.uk) is a fine website gathering together photographs and comments on prehistoric sites around the world. Created entirely by amateur enthusiasts and edited by Andy Burnham, it's absolutely fascinating and you can search for just about any type of prehistoric site you care to mention and the personal accounts give you a real feel for the atmosphere of each place.

The CD ROM *Field Guide to Megalithic Ireland* by Anthony Weir is clear and beautifully produced – it's almost as good as being there yourself. Log on to www.irishmegaliths.org.uk to find out more.

THE IRON AGE

INTRODUCTION

For archaeologists, the defining difference in this new Iron Age was, of course, the appearance of iron for tools and weapons. More readily available in Britain than copper ore, iron ore can be smelted in a furnace and forged to create stronger tools for use in the home and the fields – that's the fields of grain *and* the fields of war, for weapons were increasingly needed in a land that was filling up with hillforts. From Credenhill Camp on the Welsh borders and Eidon Hill hillfort near Melrose in Scotland, to promontory forts like that at Ness of Burgi in Shetland and Trevelgue Head in Cornwall, gatehouses and entrance defences were added to sturdy ramparts that were faced with stone and laced with timbers.

By 450 BC the population was expanding and stronger forts with double or even triple sets of ramparts were replacing the weaker, earlier versions. Tre'r Ceiri in Wales is a solid example, with one heavily built stone wall in places but double (and even treble) ramparts in others. This was a time of tribal identities and inter-tribal wars in which captured enemies regularly became slaves, long before the Romans' slave-based economy reached Britain. Vast linear earthworks such as Wheathampstead Dyke in Hertfordshire and Grim's Ditch, a 40km gash across the Chilterns, divided the land into battle-hardened territories.

Not all was war though. Some forts look very bellicose but were clearly built purely for show and prestige – the Chesters in East Lothian has impressive 5m-high ramparts but, being overlooked by a ridge, evidently had few defensive pretensions. Ramparted Danebury was actually growing into a vibrant regional centre for trade while Maiden Castle in Dorset was home for several hundred people during this time. Life undeniably continued, but mostly behind large earthworks. These communities were the nearest equivalent to Iron Age 'towns' but there were no monumental buildings, no public infrastructure and no centralised government.

In Scotland, unrest caused small thick-walled stone fortifications to spring up along the rocky west coast and the western islands. Called duns (Gaelic for 'castles') or brochs, their construction was monumental in scale and defensive in purpose. The only force that could unify such bellicose tribes was a common enemy and that arrived in the shape of the Roman legionaries in AD 43.

Historically, this invasion marked the end of the Iron Age but the old ways and traditions would rumble on long afterwards, especially in the outlying western lands: Chysauster village in Cornwall retained its traditional Iron Age roundhouses well into the occupation; Scotland and Ireland remained out of the grip of the Roman authorities and continued their own building traditions untainted by the Roman villa or bathhouse. For the other tribes, life as they knew it would never be the same again and Rome was here to stay.

◉ LOOK OUT FOR . . .

The Stone Age had its megaliths and the Bronze Age is famous for its barrows, but the Iron Age left us some of the most impressive earthworks ever to be made in Britain.

◉ **Hillforts** still dominate the land around them, even after 2000 years. There are plenty for us to find, with over 2000 officially reported forts alone, and countless others remaining unnamed and unreported. They vary immensely in size and in the number of ramparts and ditches and internal buildings. Identifying the different classes of fort is worthy of a book in itself. For our purposes though, a few pointers to recognising the main features will suffice:

Early hillforts often had just a single set of banks and ditches with one or maybe two entrances according to need.

On hilltops the boundary wall might be nothing more than roughly-built drystone walls which helped to exaggerate the already steep terrain (Ingleborough in Yorkshire, or Caer Twr in Anglesey, for example).

Some rough drystone ramparts were built to cut off a promontory, especially on the ragged coasts of Cornwall, Scotland and Ireland. Their battered bases can sometimes still be seen.

The walls around Caer Twr in Anglesey look rough and ready but they've survived for 2000 years. (© Gillian Hovell)

Hillfort defences grew ever bigger as the years passed, and some existing forts, like Almondbury hillfort in Yorkshire, grew greatly in size and acquired more ditches and banks as the need arose – Castle Ring Hillfort in Staffordshire's Cannock Chase has two banks and ditches on its steeper north side, but five on the south east where the ground is more level and prone to attack. These ramparts were more than simple piles of earth: constructed of rubble and earth piled within a timber frame, they were strengthened with wooden through-beams.

It's worth remembering that the ditches would have been twice as deep as they are now since 2000 years of gradual infilling with soil and erosion of the banks have dramatically softened the ditches' profile. Stanwick's excavated section close to Forcett Village in Yorkshire has exposed fortifications rising a daunting 5m.

Some forts grew to provide shelter for the tribe's valuable cattle. However, this made them difficult to defend and at the Brigantes stronghold of Stanwick fort you can share a moment of history. 6.5km (4 miles) of ramparts encircled over 700 acres, but their great length proved to be indefensible when Rome's Ninth legion waltzed in in AD 71.

Some forts lack any sign of habitation but inside others (such as Hod Hill in Dorset and Eidon Hill in the Scottish borders) there are roundhouses, religious shrines and storage pits. For an idea of how sophisticated life could

TOP TIP

Hillforts' regional variations: spot the differences.

Corridor entrances became common in southern England and an outer gate might be added for extra defence. Most large single-ramparted hillforts are to be found in Southern England.

In western Britain, timber guard chambers developed and, although these have long since rotted away, many were replaced by stone ones built just behind the ramparts or at the end of a corridor entrance.

In northern Britain, an easy supply of stone meant that the ramparts were often faced with stone. 'Vitrified' forts, where the stone and timber have been burned (deliberately or due to attack) so that the intense heat has fused the stone into a solid glassy mass, are common in Scotland and have been found in Northern Ireland.

Nearly half of the large multi-ramparted forts are in Dorset, Wiltshire and Hampshire, with many also in Shropshire. Most of these overlook one or more major river valleys – Hod Hill and Hambledon Hill both watch over rivers which provide access from the coast to inland chalk downs.

be inside these proto-towns, visit Danebury and as you walk around the vast arena inside the ramparts imagine the neat rows of roundhouses in streets around the interior with a main house (could it be the chief's?), together with workshops for weaving and iron-smelting, storage areas for salt, shale and raw materials, as well as granaries and threshing floors. It was the economically-active defensive settlement forts such as this that Julius Caesar referred to as *oppida*, the Latin word for 'town'.

Occasionally, the Iron Age equivalent of tank traps defended the approach to a fort. They usually feature in Scottish and Welsh fortifications and, called chevaux de frise. These knee-high lines of pointy stones prevented full scale charges and stopped the devastating enemy chariots from getting through. In southern Britain deeper ditches and steeper ramparts were used instead. It's all a matter of contours and available raw materials.

👁 **Roundhouses** were the standard house style and numerous examples survive in open rural areas of the north and west of England, Scotland and Wales Ranging from 2m to 10m across, they had wattle and daub walls, sometimes set on low stone walls. They can be found as preserved communities (as at the Mountain Huts on Anglesey) or may be discovered separately in rough moorland and pasture as extremely ruined circular stone walls (little more than stony grass mounds) with a single entrance (*colour plate 12*).

Britain is home to certain variations on the theme of a roundhouse. Crannogs were artificial islands built in southern Scotland and all over Ireland from the Bronze Age. However, a large number of excavated sites date from the Iron Age and they tell us that some timber roundhouses were built out in the lake on substantial crannogs (measuring around 16m across) of stones, stakes or brushwood. Reached by a stone causeway or a wooden bridge on piles, the house would often nestle inside a palisade, thus betraying its defensive intentions although their location certainly helped to make the most of the much sought after fertile lakeside land. Far from being a five-minute wonder, several crannogs were occupied right through the Roman period and into the medieval era. Island McHugh, a crannog on Lough Catherine in Co. Tyrone, Northern Ireland, was originally built unusually early (in the Neolithic age) and was lived on until the late sixteenth century, giving it the longest history of any known habitation site in western Europe and making it the earliest artificial island in Britain although you do have to look very carefully beyond the ruin of its medieval castle to see its prehistoric past. Evidence of similar crannog sites at the ancient lake-side villages at Meare and Glastonbury in Somerset and Bronze Age Flag Fen was an early huge crannog, using about 1 million timbers in the construction of the island.

TOP TIP

Hollow circles on aerial photographs are often the first sign of a settlement of roundhouses as the lumps and bumps on the ground can be very ephemeral.

Iron Age traditions survived into the Roman age, especially at the margins of Roman occupation. Chysauster in Cornwall is a ruined cluster of courtyard houses which were built in Roman times (second and third century AD). Each Iron Age-style roundhouse sits within its own courtyard along with a round workshop and storage huts. At Lligwy in Anglesey there is a curious blend of Roman rectangular building and two prestigious roundhouses. Clearly, the old ways died hard.

- *Underground stone storage tunnels* and chambers are called souterrains, or earthhouses in Scotland and fogous in Cornwall. They're fantastic places to explore – just don't forget a torch!

- *Where drystone walls form the field boundaries*, watch out for huge unworked irregular earthbound ('earthfast') boulders in the base of wriggly walls – walls were built by clearing rocks from the fields and piling them up between the boulders like a giant irregular dot-to-dot picture. The peninsula of Penwith in West Cornwall is full of tiny, tangled fields enclosed by such walls.

- *Banjo enclosures* occur on gentle hillsides in Hampshire, Dorset, Wiltshire and the Cotswolds. So-called because of their round shape with a single long entrance (45-90m), all edged by v-shaped ditches. Thought to be mainly for corralling livestock, few remain visible but you can visit one that is 70m across amidst the trees in Micheldever Wood in Hampshire.

When drystone walls run between earthfast boulders they could be following prehistoric wall lines. (© Gillian Hovell)

👁 **Look very closely at barrows** because just a very few aren't the usual round Bronze Age ones – some are Iron Age 'square' barrows. Many have been ploughed out and all we can see now is a shadow of the surrounding ditch, but some of these square flat-topped mounds survive in Humber and North Yorkshire, Scotland and south Essex. Distinguished by a square or rectangular quarry ditch (around 1-2m wide) around the mound, early examples measure 5-15m across (the easiest to see of the group in Broxa Forest is c.10m across and 1m high), while later ones tend to be 5m or smaller and are more closely clumped together. It is within these square barrows that the chariot (two-wheeled carts) graves have been found recently (Wetwang Slack and Pexton Moor contained traces of intact carts but others had hints of dismantled wheels and poles).

Meanwhile, in Scotland:

👁 **Duns and brochs** are windowless stone-built fortifications which are common in the Iron Age landscape of the north and west of Scotland. The archaeological world continues to debate the difference between them but, instead of getting hung up on regional variations and the niceties of their titles (which sometimes seem to be interchangeable), we can simply enjoy these wonderful monuments by recognising that there are two different styles. Duns were stone enclosures built on the rocky shores of the west coast of Scotland and the western isles. Defensive shelters for several houses, their defensive walls could tower around 3m high and enclose an area up to 20m across.

Look carefully at their entrance passages and the notches where drawbars could 'lock' the gate, and notice the guard chambers which are often set into the solid thickness of the walls on either side of the entrances. There may be signs of enclosures for several dwellings inside the walls. For a little extra adventure, seek out the island duns which squat on rocky islands in small lochs like a fortified version of a crannog. Access was, and often still is, by a causeway of heaped-up rocks (be sure to wear waterproof footwear!): Dun an Sticir on North Uist, Loch Varavat on West Lewis, and Loch of Houlland broch on Shetland are all great fun to totter across to.

Brochs were stone-built tower-like houses. They too contain many wonderful features which make the sites great fun to visit and explore. The main entrance is a long gallery passing through the double-skinned wall and flanked by a guard-chamber set into the cavity on one side. Brochs tended to have a single main inner room and were usually taller than duns, being able to rise to 9m or more in height, partly thanks to their amazing cavity wall structure which sloped inwards for added strength: two walls, about a metre apart were built and bonded together with regular stone lintels across the gap, thus creating galleries you can still sometimes walk along and even staircases within the wall which you can climb to reach a second gallery. In some cases, small rooms between the two walls can be accessed by a lintelled doorway from the ground floor of the central inner room. Ledges protruding from the inner wall supported the roof and, in taller brochs, other ledges held beams for an upper floor or floors.

Broch villages also existed. Visit the Broch of Gurness which was an amazing 8m high (although no more than 3.5m survive today) and see the remarkable small stone dwellings which encircled it and which could have housed as many as forty families. Three ramparts and ditches surrounded the village.

- ⊚ **Wheelhouses** were circular stone structures similar to the brochs but they were divided internally by short stone walls projecting out, like spokes of a wheel, from the external walls. These appear on the Western Isles and Shetland (but not on Orkney) and some are free-standing structures (like Clettraval and Sollas on North Uist and Tigh Talamhanta in Allasdale) while others are physically linked to brochs and associated with barns or byres (like Shetland's Jarlshof or Old Scatness). Without the Roman occupation to truncate the Iron Age, Scotland's brochs (such as Jarlshof in Shetland) continue as Iron Age dwellings right into the first century AD.

- ⊚ **Aisled wheelhouses** were a variation on the wheelhouse theme. Instead of walls running inwards to the centre of the broch like a wheel spoke, a circle of free-standing piers of stone were joined to the walls by stone lintels. Looking rather like a stone version of an Iron Age timber roundhouse, these are usually found on the Scottish islands. The precursors of many promontory brochs on Shetland were blockhouses. These were stone-built huts which became obsolete when more substantially defensible properties became necessary.

And in Ireland ...

- ⊚ **Cashels** – stone-built roughly circular forts sprang up from the first century AD. Frequently sited on vulnerable land, they served more as look-out posts with stone staircases, wall-chambers and terraces and as status symbols rather than defensible structures. Often used right into medieval times, many still stand watch over the sea today. Be wary of over-restored examples though, as the Victorians were keen to over-romantically renovate these sites.

Where to go

Iron Age sites are spread across all of Britain and although they are mostly forts or roundhouses, there are plenty of fascinating features for us to explore.

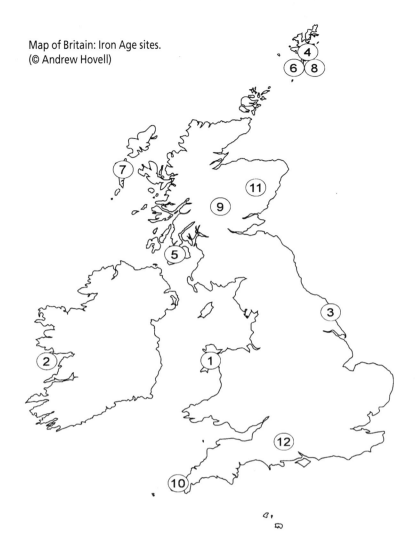

Map of Britain: Iron Age sites.
(© Andrew Hovell)

Hillforts

1 There are so many hillforts across Britain that it is impossible to pick out just one – Maiden Castle in Dorset and Danebury in Hampshire have great ramparts and entrance defences. In good weather, the views from hillforts are always great, and in the mist they are breathtakingly atmospheric. Traprain Law in East Lothian is a good one to visit in Scotland and the heavyweight Tre'r Ceiri ('Town of the Giants') on the Welsh Llyn Peninsular still has walls standing to 3m.

Chevaux de frise

2 Only a few *chevaux de frise* have been found. Dreva Craig hillfort, south of Broughton, Scotland has two stone ramparts as well as these ancient tank traps. Castell Henllys in Pembrokeshire, Wales has a section exposed by the fort entrance. Dun Aengus on Ireland's Aran islands boasts four concentric drystone walls and the spiky *chevaux de frise* lurk outside the third ring. With fine views and tales of druids, this is a gem.

Large linear earthworks

3 To see the large linear earthworks, visit Dane's Dykes where the entire peninsula of Flamborough in Yorkshire is cut off by massive earthworks. Grim's Ditch near Great Hampden runs across the Chilterns for 40 km (25 miles) and is also considered to have been built in the Iron Age.

Scottish brochs

4 To appreciate the brooding weight of the Scottish brochs you simply have to visit Mousa Broch in Shetland, even though it's much bigger than your average broch. The most complete broch in Scotland (and therefore the world) was built in the second century BC. It still stands to its full height of 13m with a walkway on top that you can reach via the original narrow and uneven curving stone steps which run up through the gap between the massive inner and outer walls. Inside the dun you can duck into three cells nestling around the central court and gaze up at their corbelled roofs. Check the weather and times of the daily summer ferry from Lerwick that will get you to this distant but fantastic monument.

TOP TIP

The best examples of typical brochs that swaggered as impressive statements of wealth and power are the Glenelg duns (Dun Telve and Dun Troddan, *colour plate 13*). Dun Carloway on Lewis is well worth visiting too, and the islands are just littered with brochs.

Dun Carloway on Lewis still impresses. (© Liz Forrest)

Duns

5 Duns are subtle features that hide within the bracken. If you're on the Scottish mainland, visit Kildonan Dun in Argyll & Bute. Look out for the steps to a vanished higher level, the door jambs and holes for a bar to lock it. Don't forget to enjoy the sea view and keep a watch for otters fishing below the rocky cliff.

Wheelhouses

6 Wheelhouses are impressive and fun properties to explore. Jarlshof on Shetland is the place to see two good examples tucked into the courtyard of an earlier broch – they survive to a height which enables us to sense just how dark and cramped it must have been once the door was barred shut.

Aisled wheelhouses

7 Aisled wheelhouses are usually found on the Scottish islands. Udal on North Uist has an excellent example of the freestanding pillars.

Blockhouses

8 Blockhouses were frequently replaced by the brochs, but you can still find traces of them nearby. At both Ness of Burgi and Loch of Huxter on Shetland, the blockhouse was incorporated into the broch as a gatehouse. The blockhouse at Burgi Geos on the remote Shetland island of Yell, has a showy but not very functional *chevaux de frise*.

Crannogs

9 Crannogs occur in southern Scotland and all over Ireland. Most of the archaeological remains are limited to double rows of darkened timber stumps marching out into a lake like some ancient jetty. However, the Scottish Crannog Centre on Loch Tay (which boasts traces of around twenty crannogs) has built an fascinating and instructive reconstruction on the 2600 year-old site of Oakbank Crannog (*colour plate 14*).

Courtyard houses

10 The courtyard houses in the settlement of Chysauster in Cornwall date from the second and third centuries AD but they retained the traditional way of life that had gone on for generations before the Romans arrived. The reconstructed house and the stone foundations of eight houses along a street give a startling glimpse into village life in the Iron Age: each single-roomed house faced away from the prevailing wind, and sat in its own enclosed yard which contained smaller sheds or pens and stone channels to supply and remove water. The houses themselves had open hearths whose smoke filtered through the thatched conical roofs. Don't miss the remains of the 'fogou' too.

Souterrains

11 You can crawl into two souterrains (earth houses) at Jarlshof while visiting the wheelhouses there, or brave dropping down the 1m square hatch into the 14m- (45ft-) long tunnel at Culsh in Grampian – it's dauntingly dark so you'll definitely need a torch to explore it.

Figsbury Ring

12 If you love mysteries, head for Figsbury Ring in Wiltshire. Listed as a single ramparted hill fort it has an inner circular ditch. An irresistible walk around the top of the ramparts with great views – and a great reminder that even the experts can't explain everything!

Figsbury Rings.
(© Gillian Hovell)

What was life like?

The Iron Age began in the grip of cooler and wetter weather. Communities were being forced to cluster together on the drier, free-draining hillside soils, perched somewhere between the peat that was spreading across the previously fertile uplands and the heavy soils of the thickly wooded valleys. The once isolated farmsteads had now given way to clustered settlements made up of roundhouses with their conical thatched roofs grouped around workshops.

Meat was rarely hunted except on the fringes of farmland now. Early breeds of sheep (similar to Soay sheep) provided the wool which formed nearly all clothing material. Domesticated cattle, pigs and even horses and dogs (which were at this time eaten more often than fish) all lived in the enclosures which covered the land. But not all these farming hamlets survived purely on hand-to-mouth subsistence farming – a 40ft-long logboat at Hasholme in the Vale of York was found sunk in a creek. Its cargo had been a substantial quantity of cuts of beef that was obviously intended for trade.

In the lowlands there was plenty of arable farming as iron enabled the heavier soils to be worked. The primitive emmer wheat gave way to spelt and, together with the new hulled barley and some beans and peas, productivity had improved. All over

Britain certain fields were landscaped into lynchet banks to make efficient terraces for extended farming.

Once harvested, the grain had to be safely stored in the cool and dry. Large pits were usually dug in the settlements and experiments have shown that the grain stored in these formed a crust which sealed it and kept the grain fresh, even in bad conditions, for months (if not years). Where conditions were not suitable for such pits, granaries raised the harvest off the damp ground.

Elsewhere, the intriguing storage systems, the earth houses (also known as souterrains or, in Cornwall, fogous) had appeared: curving underground tunnels built of and paved with stone led to underground stone-lined chambers in which grain and possibly dairy products were kept safe, cool and dry, sometimes aided by ventilation holes and drains set within the stone floor.

The grain would eventually be ground using quern stones – every home had one. Saddle querns were the earliest style and they required the grain to be back-breakingly ground by rubbing one stone back and forwards on the grain which sat in a slight hollow of a larger saddle-shaped stone placed on the floor. It was during the later Iron Age that the labour-saving devices, the beehive rotary querns, first appeared and we can almost hear the sigh of relief across the millennia – now all you had to do was rotate the user-friendly wooden handle back and forth to operate a round-topped (beehive-shaped) stone on a heavy bottom stone.

As a result of all this farming, the landscape was filled to bursting (which added to the lack of hunting) but the only major town-like settlements were the hillforts that were multiplying. Nestling in the safety of the ramparts were houses, workshops and storage pits/buildings and, in the larger forts, the livestock they depended on.

But what of the smaller settlements? In the second century BC, clusters of courtyard houses, such as Chysauster and Carn Euny developed in Cornwall. These were largely timber and wattle-and-daub structures, with durable stone foundations. Few other stone buildings were built – the only other truly stone buildings of any size that we find in pre-Roman Britain were the brochs in Northern Scotland where nearly every home was, literally, a castle. Self-sufficiency up here was vital: the archaeological remains show that hunted deer and all manner of seafood including seals, whales and seabirds supplemented the planted cereals and the domesticated sheep and cattle.

It seems that no one had an easy life in the Iron Age. Even high-status houses were much the same as those of the poor. One wealthy residence has been excavated at Birnie, near Elgin in Grampian. This roundhouse had been burned down but

Using a saddle quern. (© Neil Burridge, Bronze Age Re-enactments filming supplies)

preserved in the cold embers lay the status symbols of a bronze harness from a chariot (the sports car of its day), glass beads, an iron sword hilt, a brooch and the end knob (terminal) of a valuable gold torc. Yet even this home of status goods had a simple turf roof and was built to the same basic roundhouse design (although admittedly a little larger than normal). Possessions may have varied, but those possessions were still relatively few until the Roman decadent materialism arrived. Excavated rubbish tips (middens) contain only organic waste and the occasional unsalvageable scrap – this was no throw-away society: goods were cherished and broken pots and tools were mended or re-used and metal items melted down and recycled.

TOP TIP

Most possessions from the Iron Age have been found not in homes but in graves (mostly in south east England, Dorset and Cornwall, and East Yorkshire): decorated mirrors, expensive wooden 'buckets' (see how understated this 'bucket' name is by visiting the Marlborough Bucket at the Wiltshire Heritage Museum), jewellery, pots and swords were among the valued goods.

In the final century of the Iron Age, trade with the increasingly Romanised continent began to flourish. Iron Age coins appeared, mimicking the concept of Roman currency and the continental connections influenced the stylised and geometric motifs that made up early Celtic art (known as La Tene art) – the inhabitants of Iron Age Britain were anything but insular and those living along the international ports of the Solent coast were already familiar with Mediterranean figs, far eastern spices and even North African incense decades before the first Roman invasion in 55 BC. In return for these imports, British hunting dogs and other commodities were exported – and the Roman-made 5.5m-long slave chain from Bigbury Hillfort in Kent hints that a dark trade in human beings was either already or about to be included in this list.

Life was cheap and war was a way of life. The Britons were very proud of their war chariot skills, and harnesses and horse trappings are found throughout the Iron Age. But weaponry was sometimes ceremonial rather than battle-worthy – the Waterloo horned parade helmet was clearly for display, as was the Battersea Shield, both found in the Thames. Both seem to have been an offering to the water. There was certainly a spiritual element to Iron Age life: a single Welsh lake, Llyn Fawr, has been found to contain a decorative sword, huge cauldrons, bronze axes, razors and a sickle. The British kept no records so we have only the Roman accounts to unbalance our view of religion in Iron Age Britain. Julius Caesar's self-congratulating account of his invasion of Britain (as seen through the eye of the conqueror) wrote of druids whose religion

The most valuable item owned might have been a torc, the twisted bands of gold that were worn around the neck. Great skill was used to create them – take a good close look at one next time you see one in a museum.

required no temples but who communed with the spirits of nature. Human sacrifice was mentioned and, even though Caesar was vamping up his account for Roman sympathies, there can be no denying the existence of six skulls found in the wooden gateway at Bredon Hill fort or the human skulls in the Danebury pits. And what of Lindow Man, found struck twice on the head, garrotted, neck broken, knifed in the throat and left face-down in a bog in the years soon after the invasion? While he may simply have been loathed and earned some horrific vengeance, archaeologists agree that this overkill almost certainly bears witness to ritual sacrifice.

Ritual undoubtedly played an important part in Iron Age life. Parts of animals and even of humans are buried in strategic places (especially pits and ditches) in many settlements. An elaborate layered offering at a feast site shows that there must have been significant symbolic meaning to these deposits – but without any written records we can only guess at their meaning.

We know equally little about the rituals that accompanied death in the early years of the Iron Age – all we have are a few cremations (some in urns, some merely deposited) placed in cemeteries or under small barrows or even set in the sides of second-hand barrows that were already centuries old. However, from the fifth century BC burials appear in the south and east, in isolated burials and in the west and north of Britain in stone boxes called cists or in cemeteries with a few grave goods. Basically, it seems that anything was acceptable: bodies were exposed on platforms until the bare disarticulated bones could be dropped into shallow graves or scattered in pits and ditches, or they were cremated or buried (both with or without grave goods) in stone cists, wooden coffins or beneath small barrows. However, one distinct group of burials have been found in North East England – the cart burials – where a dismantled chariot or cart was laid in a large square barrow (as in East Yorkshire's Great Driffield burial and Danes' Graves in the Vale of York, as well as in North Humberside's Garton-on-the-Wolds and Wetwang Slack). Iron Age life may have been brutal and tough, but it evidently still had meaning.

The hillforts and brochs speak loudly of violent times. Iron produced not just tools but weapons: the clashing of iron swords gave way to silent daggers for a while but in the third century BC swords, socketed spearheads and iron arrowheads made their mark and it was they that greeted the invaders from Rome. Yet bronze still had its place, as can be seen in finds like the Deskford Carnyx, the war trumpet cast like an animal head which bellowed a haunting welcome to the invading Roman army.

Things to do

The Iron Age may not have left a lot of artefacts for us to find, but there is enough for us to get a good idea of what life was like and to 'reconstruct' how we think it might have been.

Experimental archaeology is a crucial way to 'fill the gaps' in our knowledge. Butser Ancient Farm near Petersfield in Hampshire does this on a grand scale. This is not a museum or a theme park but a serious major research programme which has been running since 1972. The reconstructed roundhouses (*colour plate 15*) have taught us that they were a stunningly efficient design, well-built and often spacious – (which makes sense or why else would it have been the preferred design for thousands of years since the Bronze Age). The working farm has gathered data about the ancient breeds of sheep and game, and the earliest wheat crops – again, Iron Age farming was far more efficient than we might expect. With demonstrations in ancient skills such as forging iron, wattle work and wood turning this is an excellent place for dispelling any preconceived ideas of the Iron Age being a primitive era.

Castell Henllys hillfort in the Pembrokeshire Coast National Park is another reconstruction site, but with a difference – these roundhouses are built *in situ*, on the very same foundations as the original roundhouses of 200 BC. This was the fort that was used for the BBC's *Surviving the Iron Age* in 2001. It's all very atmospheric and some helpful information boards set the scene as you troll up from the shop and entrance at the bottom of the hill. Once through the single entrance to this little fort, and past the excavated *chevaux de frise*, you can wander around the refurnished huts, watch ancient wood turning and, on certain days, listen to the storyteller showing children how to be an Iron Age warrior or bread-maker. Very informative and all good stuff.

The Archaeolink Prehistoric Park in Aberdeenshire takes us right up to the end of Prehistory with another reconstructed Iron Age roundhouse and a working farmstead with livestock and crops. It's all based on an excavation near the Aberdeenshire village of Monymusk. Here you can be transported back in time and watch demonstrations of pottery, ancient cooking and spinning and weaving. Go to www.archaeolink.co.uk

The Scottish Crannog Centre on Loch Tay has a reconstructed Iron Age loch-dwelling which was built by the Scottish Trust for Underwater Archaeology (STUA) who continue to explore similar sites in the area and run summer field schools on

Reconstructed roundhouse.
(© Archaeolink Prehistory Park)

underwater archaeology: the on-site exhibition shows videos which take you through the amazing underwater excavations and the experimental building of the crannog (so you can see if this very special branch of archaeology might be for you!). The exhibition also contains the original artefacts and evidence for the peaceful and successful crannog life which was surprisingly sophisticated and comfortable. Experimental archaeology is at the heart of this site and you can try your hand at the ancient skills of woodworking, bow-drilling and grinding flour.

To picture life in a hillfort, visit the Museum of the Iron Age at Andover which is largely devoted to bringing alive the finds from the Danebury excavations. A research room, full of archaeological resources, is available for public use. Finds from other major sites are displayed in local museums: Dorset County Museum in Dorchester houses much of material excavated at Maiden Castle while Hull & East Riding Museum has many of the wonderful finds from Iron Age burials in the region.

TOP TIP

To sample the riches of the Iron Age, see:

the Llyn Cerig Bach hoard of iron objects in the National Museum of Wales;

the Waterloo Helmet and Battersea Shield in the British Museum;

the gold Broighter torc in the National Museum of Ireland;

the Deskford Carnyx in the National Museum of Scotland.

For a glimpse into death in the Iron Age, visit the British Museum where 'the body in the bog', Lindow Man, now rests in a quiet corner of the second floor gallery. Close to other Iron Age grave-related items from various sites (including a chariot wheel from the cart burial at Garton Station, East Yorkshire, c.300-200 BC), this is an ideal place to contemplate various Iron Age burial styles.

As the Iron Age runs into the Roman period, the family-orientated *Vicus* re-enactment society combines experimental archaeology and reconstruction with family fun and public and private events that cover both the Roman advance and the native response. Dig out www.vicus.org.uk for more information.

Reading up

There are numerous books on the Iron Age which are often listed under titles involving the native 'Celts'). *The Ancient Celts* by Barry Cunliffe (Penguin Books Ltd 1999) and *Britain and the Celtic Iron Age* by Simon James and Valerie Rigby (British Museum).

More academic is Barry Cunliffe's detailed work on *Iron Age Communities in Britain* (third edition, Routledge 1991) but a summarised version is available in his *Iron Age Britain* (Batsford & English Heritage 2004). *Britain BC: Life in Britain and Ireland before the*

Romans by Francis Pryor (Harper Perennial 2004) is a very readable, if large, introduction to all of prehistory in Britain.

For information on Iron Age sites around Britain, consult the Ordnance Survey Historical Map and Guide – Ancient Britain (OS 1990), *Discovering Archaeology in England and Wales* by J. Dyer (Shire 1997) and *A Guide to Early Celtic Ruins in Britain* by P. Beresford Ellis (Constable 1991). Virtually all individual sites have guidebooks in some form, although *Danebury* by Barry Cunliffe (English Heritage/Batsford) gives a more detailed accoun of the excavations of this important site. www.gallica.co.uk is an enthusiasts' website which welcomes you to the 'World of the Ancient Britons', giving information on all aspects of Iron Age life – plus a handy glossary. They also provide links to its sister sites, the award-winning Association for Portland Archaeology, Building a Roman Villa at Butser Ancient Farm, Meare Lake Village Glastonbury, Ancient Music on the Aquincum Organ and the buildings at Butser Ancient Farm. For the teachers amongst you, they include a school special 'The Adventures of Bran' (an Iron Age boy).

TOP TIP

To get more visitor information on individual sites, check out the site websites as well as the websites and members' guidebooks for national institutions such as English Heritage, the National Trust and Historic Scotland. Wales' CADW have published a region by region four-volume Guide to Ancient and Historic Wales.

THE ROMANS

INTRODUCTION: A Potted History of Roman Britain

When Julius Caesar landed on the south coast of Britain in 55 BC, he arrived in a land of hillforts, tribes and druids. It was also a place rich in resources and goods such as tin, hunting dogs and slaves who had been already been traded across the channel for many years. However, it was also still a prehistoric society, that is, one where writing did not yet set down and record the thoughts, aspirations, politics, laws or religion of its people.

Rome, on the other hand, was at the height of its classical Golden Age: the great writers were reaching their peak and the Roman way of life was spreading in an iron grip across the continents. The traditional Roman concept that military conquest was an essential part of political success prompted Julius Caesar's brief invasions in 55 and 54 BC: it was a stepping stone for his rise to dictatorship which would, in turn, set the scene for a dynasty of Caesars who would rule the Empire. For 400 years, that Empire would include Britain – the Emperor Claudius was in need of a political boost in AD 43 and Britain offered the ideal chance for conquest and its attendant glory.

Forty thousand troops landed at Richborough in Kent, established a base of forts and promptly marched north. After the decisive victory on the Medway, Claudius himself arrived and made a triumphal entry into Colchester, complete with elephants to wow the locals before leaving his legions and the governor, Plautius (who had led the invasion), to subdue the rest of the country.

Many tribal rulers submitted and became client kingdoms of Rome (thereby enriching their own positions and coffers). As early as AD 47, Roman troops were patrolling a fortified frontier line which ran along The Fosse, from Seaton in Devon, through Bath, Cirencester, Leicester, Newark and Lincoln. By AD 51, the legions were advancing into central Wales but it wasn't until AD 61 that a new governor, a distinguished commander, Suetonius Paulinus, pushed into North Wales and smashed the druids' powerbase on Anglesey.

Then it all went horribly wrong for the Romans: when the king of the Iceni tribe died, Nero ordered his lands to be taken as a Roman province and this was done with over-enthusiastic energy and cruelty: amongst the many atrocities the king's widow, Boudicca (aka Boadicea) and her daughters were raped, sparking a revolt which almost ended Rome's hold over Britain: the Roman towns of Colchester, London and Verulamium were burned and the inhabitants were massacred – as many as 70,000 may have been killed, and Rome's Ninth Legion was annihilated before Paulinus managed to march back from Wales and finally crush the rebels.

The surviving general of the Ninth Legion went on to conquer the troubled north of Britain, establishing the re-manned Ninth Legion at Eboracum (York). Later, the commander Agricola moved further north, even into Scotland, defeating the gathered Caledonian forces at *Mons Graupius* in AD 84 at an, as yet, undiscovered site somewhere near Inverness. He could have gone on to consolidate this victory but the troops were recalled to hold the Rhine and Danube borders on the continent, and Rome's tentative grip on Scotland slipped from her grasp.

Emperor Hadrian then formalised the northern boundary that grew up: his Wall was completed in AD 122 and stretched 73 stony miles between the Solway and the Tyne. Three metres thick and nigh on seven metres high, it was manned by forts along its length which in turn were linked by mile-castles and signal towers.

In AD 140-3, the Emperor Antoninus Pius pushed forward again, building a 37-mile long turf and clay wall between the Forth and Clyde. But it couldn't last and in AD around 180 northern tribes swept over it. By the end of the century Hadrian's Wall was also wrecked as the tribes attacked the forts and wall sections. It was easy-picking as the wall was poorly manned at the time – troops had been whisked away on a doomed glory-seeking advance south by a governor who had (briefly and futilely) fancied himself as Emperor.

It is Septimus Severus' later repairs to the walls and forts in the early 200s AD which can often be seen today. A few scattered finds from his revenge expedition into the highlands of Scotland can also be found. Although Scotland was never really occupied, peace did follow for almost a century and towns and villas in Roman Britain flourished.

At the end of the third century, Saxon and Frankish pirates became troublesome in the south and the commander of the fleet, Carausius, cleared the channel, opportunistically kept the pirates' loot and then set himself up as an Emperor, ruling (effectively it has to be said) Britain and part of Gaul as an independent Empire from 286/287. But he was murdered and, in AD 296 Constantius killed his usurper and built new forts on both the 'Saxon shore' against the channel raiders and on the west coast against the Scots of Ireland. Although, or perhaps because Britain was thriving and prosperous all three frontiers continued to be gnawed at by raiders for another century.

In the early AD 400s, Rome herself came under serious threat from the Goths and troops were called back from Britain to help to protect their fatherland. In 410, the citizens of Britain sent a letter to the Emperor Honorius asking for his aid against the Saxon invaders. But Rome was already stretched to the limit and he wrote back telling them to 'look to their own defences'. Britain was now at the raiders' mercy: Roman authority and its occupying forces had left Britain for good.

◉ LOOK OUT FOR . . .

Britain was occupied by the Romans for 400 years and in that time they left plenty of evidence of the might of Rome for us to find nearly 2000 years later: stone buildings, material goods, written documents ... compared with prehistoric remains, Roman archaeology is an absolute treasure chest of goodies.

The Roman era here began as a military expedition, so let's start with the remains left by the Roman armies. Stationed across every part of Britain throughout the occupation, they left their mark in a variety of ways.

◉ **Marching camps** protected by ramparts and topped by timber palisades were built by legionaries as they swept over the land. The temporary nature of these en-route stations means that there is little impact on the ground and they can often only be discovered as faint lines on aerial photographs. Sometimes though, we can see the tell-tale rounded-cornered playing card ramparts – Mastiles Lane on the high and rough Yorkshire Malhamdale plateau passes right through one such camp and the 0.5m high x 5m wide remains of the rampart are still just visible.

◉ **Forts** were the real military base of Rome's might. Constructed quickly and without fuss, they contained set standard features which we can find today. The northern frontier lands of Hadrian's Wall are ideal places to explore their regular layouts with their central *principia* (headquarters) containing the shrine and an underground strong room for the safe storage of the soldiers' pay. The vast and substantially buttressed granaries with their drying air channels beneath them are very solid and permanent-looking features. Look out too for a (very) public toilet block and the soldiers' accommodation blocks – the best to be seen are at Caerleon

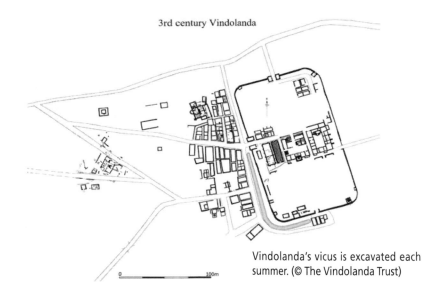

Vindolanda's vicus is excavated each summer. (© The Vindolanda Trust)

fort in South Wales. All these were laid out in a regular grid inside the rectangular but again round-cornered (playing-card shape) stone walls which were punctured by a strong gate in the centre of each side.

A thriving *vicus* often grew up outside many forts. Here soldiers' (unofficial) families lived and local traders lived and made a profit from the troops' needs. Grassy rectangular lumps and bumps outside a fort gate are usually the only signs of such a *vicus* but every summer you can watch one being excavated at Vindolanda in Northumberland.

Mile-castles were manned posts placed at intervals along Hadrian's Wall. Much smaller than forts, they only contained a small barrack block and a kitchen. One of the best preserved is Poltross Burn Milecastle, just five minutes walk from Gilsland Station. Inside its ruined wall you can see the kitchen's oven and the first of the stairs that the soldiers climbed to the wall-walk.

Turrets were placed between milecastles as look-out posts and signal stations, and their steps also gave access to the wall-walk. The remains of Banks East Turret near Birdoswald Fort is conveniently beside the modern road while

The solid granary buttresses at Vindolanda Fort. (© Gillian Hovell)

Brunton Turret still stands over 2.5m (8ft) high in places. Look closely at 'The Wall' here and you can see the original 10ft wide foundations jutting out from the narrower wall that was eventually built on top – was the stone or money running out or was the work slipping behind schedule and speed meant cutting back?

Shore forts. Raids from abroad in the late third century and the fourth century prompted the building of the defensive Saxon shore forts along the south and east coasts of England. Look for the stone walls with bonding courses of tiles set into walls of irregular shaped stones (like flint), and evidence of round bastions which once supported ballistae (catapults). There may be partly filled-in remains of a single ditch which bounded the fort and you will find a single entrance in the middle of one side. Be aware though that other features you find may not be Roman – being placed at key strategic points these forts were often reused throughout the next millennium, especially by the Normans and as twentieth-century coastal defence sites.

Military roads connected all Roman forts and towns. Although some remained in use and now have a modern road over it (Watling Street is now the A5) and a map may mark up a brief section of suspected or known 'Roman road', many fell from use. Finding Roman roads is a tricky past-time. It's a fallacy that all Roman roads were straight (they often worked around awkward contours) but they contrasted with most rough roads that went before as they certainly had long straight sections. It's perhaps worth checking for artificially straight, compacted, cambered (and guttered) hints of tracks along the lines between known strategic Roman sites but it's almost impossible to be sure about them – it's a fun game though!

Of course, the story of Roman Britain is not just a military one:

Country villas were soon fashionable replacements for even the grandest Iron Age roundhouse. Over the years they gradually became more prosperous, growing in size and sporting mosaic floors and ever posher bathhouses. A few were even built in reluctant Wales (the largest is at Llantwith Major, with another at Ely near Cardiff and three more near Caerwent). Naturally, every villa was different but here is a very rough guide to dating features in villas:

Villas which were little more than a corridor with rooms opening off it were built early in the occupation.

Wall-paintings were regular features in many villas after the middle of the first century AD and fragments of wall plaster coloured by red and yellow ochre, red iron oxide, powdered charcoal and copper silicate sometimes survive (*colour plate 16*).

Winged corridor houses were very common in Britain after AD 100 and are recognisable as a corridor with rooms behind it and two wings of rooms on either side of an open courtyard. They often boasted status symbols such as mosaic floors, bath suites with hypocausts and additional outbuildings.

Mosaics would later be replaced with newer, more fashionable designs: a new one would be laid on top of the old, like new kitchen lino. Where you see an old mosaic poking out below another, notice the change in fashions: was one black and white geometric patterns while the other bragged the fancy new colour pictorial images (*colour plate 17*).

The richest villas in Britain – the courtyard villas – had rooms surrounding all four sides of a courtyard. You can usually be sure that these date to the second or third century.

Rectangular aisled houses now appear on wealthy estates. Posts divided the building into a central nave with two aisles and they may have bath suites with hypocausts and mosaics for us to look for.

A number of villas fell from use during the troubled third century: villas in the south were especially vulnerable. Even Fishbourne's grand villa may have been deserted at this time, while Dover's Painted House (built around AD 200) was demolished by the Roman army to make way for essential military works and it was buried beneath a fort.

In the fourth century many villas were abandoned and as Rome retreated in the early fifth century the last remaining villas fell into disrepair: hearths and posts were dug into old mosaic floors when the ruinous shell of the building was still used as a rough hovel.

The Romans created not just the new country house culture but an urban society previously unseen in Britain. Surrounded by solid walls and containing public buildings many have now been built over but there are remains of certain features we can still visit – most private homes may have gone but the bath houses with their underfloor heating 'hypocausts', amphitheatres and monuments were all built to last.

- 👁 **Amphitheatres** were the major public centres of entertainment and could take thousands of spectators on their tiered seats. Gladiatorial fights and animal shows drew the crowds here – this was the dark side of Roman life.
- 👁 **Monumental arches** are rare in Britain but a visit to Richborough (*Rutupiae*) castle in Kent will give a good sense of the dramatic impression the arch was designed to make: the solid cross-shaped flints-set-in-mortar foundations are all that remain of the ceremonial archway built in around 85 AD but they measure a massive 40m wide and 9m deep.
- 👁 **Religion.** Burials were strictly out of town affairs and their style was all down to personal preference. Although there was a general tendency for cremations until the mid second century when burials became more common, there were no set rules: cremation or burials; prone, decapitated, or multiple burials; grave goods or not; shrouds vs. wood or lead coffins,

who cared? We can't spot these on the surface of the land but you can easily identify Roman gravestones in museums – look for the Latin inscription *DM*, a standard abbreviation of *dis manibus* ('to the spirits of the dead').

While the Iron Age Britons had worshipped in groves and the open air, the Romans built temples, shrines and stone altars and, after Christianity was introduced, chapels. So how can we recognise these religious buildings?

Classical temples were a *cella*, a simple internal room with a shrine, surrounded by a portico of columns. Excavation is the only real identifier of temples as most are now little more than foundations – see the square temples at Jordan Hill in Weymouth or Vindolanda's temple in the vicus and Hayling Island's unusual circular shrine in a square temple. Thankfully, stone altars with scroll shaped tops and Latin inscriptions to a particular god or gods give the game away and you can see these in many museums. However, temples to the eastern god, Mithras, were different. His temples can be identified by a sculpture or painting of Mithras as he cut the throat of the primeval bull in a cave so that its life force could give birth to plants and animals. His shrine, a *mithraeum*, would be small (to echo the dark cave) or sited in a dark, cave-like vaulted cellar. Traces of 'ordeal pits' used here can sometimes be seen. Soldiers were frequently his followers, responding as they did to his demands for discipline, ordeals and a progression through the mysteries of the faith and so these temples are often near forts such as Carrowburgh and Housesteads along Hadrian's Wall.

Some Romano-British villas house a very different kind of religious space – a chapel which can be identified by its Christian symbols. A Greek symbol which looks like a large 'X' with a 'P' cutting through it is a sure sign of Christianity being worshipped here: the X was the 'chi' (the Greek letter for 'ch') and the 'P' was a 'rho' (r) and this special combination stood for the first letters of 'Christ'. Similarly, the depiction of a fish was a secret sign for Christians who feared persecution as the Greek letters which make up *ichthys* ('fish' in Greek) were used as an acronym, each letter standing for a different Greek word which together in English mean 'Jesus Christ Son of God, Saviour'. Both symbols continued to be used in the fifth century when the Emperor Constantine made Christianity the Empire's official religion and they are still used in modern churches and by Christians today.

Where to go

Virtually any Roman site is a treat to visit. At some of them you can almost hear the bark of the centurion's orders and the tramp of the Roman hob-nailed boots on the paving. To get a fuller picture of life under Rome though, it's worth visiting a broad spectrum of Roman archaeological remains and here are twelve of the best to get you started.

Instead of simply using a Sat. Nav. whenever you go somewhere new, check the OS map. There is a good chance a Roman road or fort may be marked along your route.

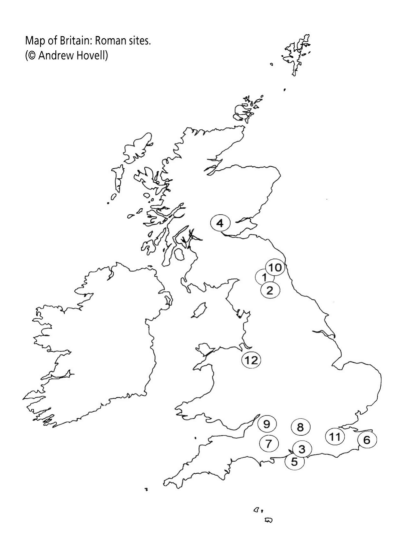

Map of Britain: Roman sites.
(© Andrew Hovell)

Hadrian's Wall

1 To feel the force of the Roman army, visit Hadrian's Wall – now a World Heritage Site – and walk round Housesteads Fort. Once through the National Trust shop you scale the slopes to the magnificent walls enclosing the raised granaries, barracks, paved floors, hospital and the ever-popular ancient flushing toilets. Head west along the sheer crags on foot for about ten minutes, exploring Milecastle 39 en route, and then turn and enjoy a classic iconic image of Hadrian's Wall and let your imagination do the rest (*colour plate 18*).

Vindolanda

2 Unfortunately, the vicus that sprang up around many a fort is rarely well excavated or displayed, being limited to a few grassy humps and bumps. At Vindolanda, just south of the Wall, it's different: you can see whole building walls, excavated houses, baths with hypocausts, temple outlines, drainage systems and paved roads. This, combined with a visit to the sister site a short drive down the road, the Roman Army Museum, is the place to get a sense of the lively buzz of activity that once surrounded the military bases.

Porchester Castle

3 Portchester Castle in Hampshire was the most western of the Saxon shore forts. Built c.260 AD it has a complicated mass of ruins including a Norman castle inside it but the walls are nonetheless possibly the best preserved Roman fort walls in Northern Europe. You can even spot the change in builder gangs as you look along the full circuit of walls which rise to their full height of 5m (27ft). Rounded hollow D-shaped bastions were bases for light catapults which stood on long-vanished timber floors. See also Richborough's Castle Fort in Kent and Burgh Castle's walls in Norfolk.

Ardoch Fort

4 Scotland was never conquered by the Romans, but that wasn't from lack of trying – if they hadn't been recalled after their decisive victory at *Mons Graupius* the story could have been very different. As it is though, there are few Roman sites in Scotland but a series of forts were built along the Gask Ridge between Dunblane and Perth. Ardoch Fort was built in that first push forward and re-occupied in the Emperor Antonius Pius' advance in the AD 140s. Despite the lack of building ruins, the earthworks are most impressive, with five ditches in places and it's well worth a visit.

Ardoch Fort's earthworks remain easily visible, even 2000 years on. (© Liz Forrest)

Brading Roman Villa

5 Most Roman villas can be found in the fertile south east lowlands of England. One of the best is Brading Roman Villa, on the Isle of Wight. The villa itself has some great mosaics and is wonderfully presented in its award-winning exhibition and visitor centre with plenty of fascinating information and an extensive range of archaeology to investigate. See www.bradingromanvilla.org.uk for more details. Other great villas are Fishbourne and Bignor in Sussex with their stunning mosaics.

Painted House

6 Sections of twenty-eight panels of decorated plaster can be seen in the Painted House in Dover (*Dubris*) (*colour plate 19*). Totalling 400 sq ft, they have remarkably survived by being buried under the ramparts of a later Saxon shore fort. The house may have been a *mansio* (an overnight lodge for Roman-friendly travellers) and the exhibition here superbly tells the story of the excavation and discoveries. You also get to see part of the fort's wall and a hefty bastion.

Ackling Dyke Roman Road

7 The very best preserved example of a road with its raised *agger* (cambered causeway) and drainage ditches down both sides is Ackling Dyke Roman Road in Dorset. The Roman road still runs several miles along a track way which heads straight towards the hillfort at Bradbury Rings along a public right of way (off the B3081) and it actually drives straight through the Oakley Down group of Bronze Age bowl, disc and bell barrows.

Silchester

8 Not only did the Romans bring urban life to Britain, but they built walls around the towns. Many modern towns built on Roman ones still have relics of those walls hidden within their modern streets – seek them out in Exeter, Colchester and Canterbury among others, along with a 20ft-high stretch near the Tower of London. However, for a complete, if crumbly, 2.5-km (1.5m-) circuit of town walls, visit Silchester in Hampshire. It's somewhat surreal as the walls now encircle empty fields but they were built mostly from the 200s AD and the town flourished even after the Romans left before being totally abandoned. While you're there, take a look at the ruins of the amphitheatre, set as usual, just outside the walls: over 4500 spectators watched shows here.

The towering Silchester Walls surround nothing but an empty field now. (© Andrew Hovell)

Bath

9 Of course, the ultimate Roman bath is the splendid (if busy) complex in the heart of the City of Bath (*Aquae Sulis* to the Romans). Built on the site of the existing hot springs that were sacred to the Celtic goddess, Sul, the Romans did what they did best: they made it their own. Peer through a Roman arch at the sacred spring and tread on the very stones the Roman walked on around the great bath which is still lined with lead and filled with that green hot spa water. Follow the East Baths' sequence of changing rooms, pool and heated rooms where decorated walls have been suspended over the original foundations to give a sense of how huge it once was. And tour the West Baths' heated pools and rooms with their hypocaust system but prepare to shiver as you feel the cold air above the circular 1.6m deep cold plunge bath. It's all very evocative and you feel that at any moment a Roman senator will amble through – which they do on certain afternoons! (www.romanbaths.co.uk)

Carrowburgh

10 To see a Mithraeum temple visit the ruins at Carrowburgh along the B6318 on Hadrian's Wall, and see a colourful reconstruction of it in the Great North Museum of Antiquities. For those who aren't in the neighbourhood, virtual tours of the ruins and the reconstructed Mithraeum are hosted on www.museums.ncl.ac.uk

Lullingstone Villa

11 For early evidence of early Christianity in a Roman setting, head to Lullingstone Villa near Eynsford in Kent. First built in AD 75, it was, like so many villas, 'modernised' in later centuries. As well as its famous fourth-century mosaics of the *Rape of Europa* and *Bellerophon riding Pegasus* (which includes swastika motifs) and the contemporary bath house which was undoubtedly built to impress, the cellar of this vast villa turns out to be a Christian chapel, complete with some of the earliest Christian wall paintings in Britain. Intriguingly, the same room contains earlier pagan wall paintings of two water nymphs which had been covered over. While you're there, don't miss the mausoleum, kitchen and the substantial raised granary for a complete Roman experience.

Amphitheatres

12 Dramatic amphitheatres still exist at St Albans and Caerleon, while Chester's (where 10,000 could watch the shows) is surrounded by a modern road. Silchester's amphitheatre sits outside the Roman town walls in a peaceful spot which belies the violent activities that once went on here.

What was life like?

There can be no denying that the Iron Age Britons and the invading Romans were poles apart in lifestyles. The native tribes were fractious and lived in

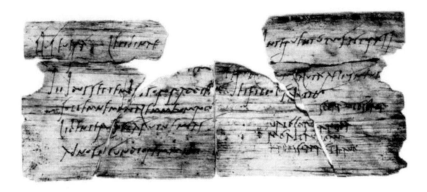

One of the Vindolanda writing tablets that tell us so much about life on the frontier and which were named the British Museum's Top Treasure – this one is a birthday invitation. (© Vindolanda Trust)

clusters of smoky roundhouses with few possessions. The Romans on the other hand were practiced city-dwellers who washed daily and whose elite lived in clean-cut, luxury-filled centrally heated houses while their soldiers were drilled in obedience in the ranks. Was it any wonder that the local magnates, faced with the traditional Roman option of annihilation or receiving a few tasty privileges from a rich and powerful Roman master, chose to throw in their lot with the invaders?

For those who eased the rapid onward path of the legions, life moved from prehistory into bureaucracy in one fell swoop. The writing tablets from Vindolanda show that every soldier's movements were accounted for and supplies were minutely logged. No doubt the same enthusiasm for precision reporting reached other areas of life – 'paperwork' had entered Britain, albeit on wax and wooden tablets.

If the rewards for subservience to a foreign ruler and his civil service were great, the price was still high. Hobnobbing with the powers-that-be meant speaking Latin, taking a Latin name and adopting a new style of dress and community living – in essence, it meant abandoning the old ways. A few outposts, like Chysauster in Cornwall and the amazing half-native, half-Roman Lligwy in Anglesey, clung to their traditional roundhouses but, elsewhere, ordered straight lines now ruled: houses were rectangular and roads powered straight across the land, linking strategic points such as forts and towns. A few villas can be found even in reluctant Wales (the largest is at Llantwith Major, with another at Ely near Cardiff and three more near Caerwent) and Latin words were absorbed into the Welsh language proving there was a blending of cultures even here.

Roman towns provided seething trading centres for both necessities and luxuries, like the new fine tableware that the recent invention of the potter's wheel was putting on the table of the rich. This was the red glossy Samian ware from France, the Wedgewood of its day, which was so popular that archaeologists have found 'fake' Samianware (a precursor to our own fake designer goods) which was perfect for a spot of very Roman social climbing.

Materialism was rife. Archaeologists scratch around for any finds from earlier eras – a broken brooch will do – until the Romans appear and then, whoosh, we're awash with fragments of pottery, gaming pieces, jewellery, glass, toilet accessories, statues and miniature statues, lead piping, a multitude of metal weapons and tools, to name just a few items. Of course, technically, the Roman era is still the Iron Age: Pliny, the great Roman writer cried that 'we have taught iron how to fly and have given it wings' for it was iron weapons that led the army's path across the world.

The political ambition that drove Rome to war was also responsible for the grand public buildings whose remains we still gaze at today. Building schemes (which would, of course, include bragging inscriptions proclaiming your glory) were one way of currying favour with the people and gaining personal success – so were the amphitheatres' free grandiose shows that political wannabes were expected to stump up buckets of cash to pay for. It was in these shows that the Roman blood lust and their innate sense of superiority over other human beings were demonstrated, fed and given a veneer of respectability. Yet it has to be admitted that the local natives had also never been shy about owning slaves, sticking their enemies' head on gateposts or, if the rumours were true, human sacrifice. 'Human rights' were a concept neither side had ever had much truck with.

Nonetheless, Roman town life had rules and it thrived. Of course, it had its downside too: there was graffiti exposing the obsessions of the locals as they scrawled fanatical support for their favourite chariot teams, declared love or hurled obscenities. In the absence of a police force crime thrived. Thefts of clothes from bath changing rooms was a hazard of life which prompted curses on a multitude of lead tablets like the ones found in Bath. And while sewers and running water may have prevented mass disease you still had to watch your step in the street to avoid the muck from cart-pulling animals and the locals' toilet-less houses. The Roman concept of civilisation was far from perfect.

For the poorer folk within the Empire, life in the army was a good opt-out clause: it gave stability, freedom from hunger, brotherhood with your compatriots (whole legions were made up of one nationality) and a promise of a pension after twenty-five years' service in the form of valuable legal rights as a Roman Citizenship and a piece of local land on which to settle down with your family.

For the civilians, Rome left you get on with life, provided you kept the peace with those who mattered, paid your taxes and gave lip service to the Emperor's cult – refuse to do the latter and you were rejecting the power of Rome. Christians' refusal to pray to the Emperor was the main cause of their clash with Rome – the Romans simply couldn't understand what the fuss was about: the Romans after all accepted all gods as worth praying to (in a 'you scratch my back and I'll scratch yours' kind of way). Gods were everywhere, in every tree, every stream and every mountain and you acknowledged them or risked a thunderbolt or similar vengeance. Even when Christianity was adopted (and legalised by Constantine's Edict of Milan in AD 313) it seems to have been viewed as an extra add-on to the all-encompassing pantheon of ubiquitous gods. The native Britons had understood about ubiquitous spirits: the only real difference was that the Romans built rather more substantial temples to their gods.

However, the arrival of the Romans had undoubtedly been a huge culture shock for the local Iron Age inhabitants. True, those on the south coast at least had traded with the continent for decades before the invasion and they must have known what was coming. But the Romans rewrote Britain's concept of society: it became unified for the first time under one all-powerful administration, rural life was taken over by the dominance of towns, and material goods flooded the land, changing the old social dynamics. however, once an accepted blend of Romano-British ideas had been established life remained relatively stable for centuries – Rome was a truly conservative society. Building fashions came and went but nothing fundamental was altered.

And yet we have to remember that, despite its dominance, Rome always remained an occupying force. Her legions watched guard from their forts for 400 years. When they were withdrawn in the early fifth century the patterns of Roman life rapidly frayed and unravelled: it had never become the warp and weft of British society – without the soldiers the old tribal factions soon raised their heads and, with no one to hobnob with, the towns and villas were abandoned and were left to fall into ruin. Rural life was back. Literacy no longer mattered. With new raiders hammering on the doors, a new culture was about to step over the threshold.

Things to do

Roman archaeological sites have an attraction all of their own, but there are many other ways of exploring the Romans' time in Britain: museums now excel in presenting their stories; excavations can be watched or even joined; responsible reconstructions are multiplying; and re-enactment events thrill with swordsmanship, costume, Roman paraphernalia and information galore.

Arbeia in South Shields has the lot. It claims to be the most extensively excavated Roman military supply base in the Empire and you can still see the classic headquarter buildings, barracks, granaries, gateways and latrines which always feature in a fort, as well as visit the site museum which houses the finds excavated here. This is a fantastic site for seeing stunning reconstructions of a gateway, the Commanding Officer's house and a barrack block, all built on their original foundations. You can also play in the hands-on archaeology *Time Quest* gallery, complete with a mock excavation with identification and sorting of artefacts, or follow the multi-sensory tour around the site. A varied diary of events takes place here, so check out their website, www.twmuseums.org.uk/arbeia or telephone 0191 456 1369 before you go to make the most of your trip.

Vindolanda's site museum is enough to make you realise that the Romans, for all their conquest and blood-letting amphitheatres, were still human after all. It's full of artefacts found on site, including the only surviving horsehair crest from a Roman helmet and an amazing and rare range of leather shoes from a posh lady's designer sandal to a baby's dainty first shoe – all uniquely preserved thanks to the rare anaerobic soggy site conditions. The site also boasts a research-driven full-size reconstruction of a wooden turret, a stone turret and a section of Wall, as well as some audio-visual reconstructed scenes under cover near the museum. A word of warning though: the enthusiasm in the film about the famous writing tablets is highly contagious and the display is fascinating but to see a collection of the tablets you need to visit the British Museum in London.

In the summer months, Vindolanda is also the place to watch excavations of the fort and the vicus being carried out. You can chat to the team and even investigate the possibility of joining them and digging there yourself. Vindolanda's sister site, the Roman Army Museum is more exciting than it sounds. It's a great place to start your voyage of discovery along The Wall: take a virtual flight over Hadrian's Wall in the *Eagle's Eye* film, see the dating strata of archaeology explained, and view a host of artefacts which give a valuable insight into life at the frontier. The main museum for Hadrian's Wall is the not-too-distant Museum of Antiquities in Newcastle-upon-Tyne's University (www.museums.ncl.ac.uk). Segedunum fort has been excavated and has a large interactive museum and a high tower for great views across its World Heritage Site.

Re-enactment groups bring history to life. The Ermine Street Guard are the foremost Roman group in the country, having mixed very real reconstructive archaeology with drama and style since 1972 – Chris Haines, the *Centurion* of the Guard, received the MBE for the Guard's service to Roman history. Anyone can join this dedicated band and, if you can't join them, you can watch them in action at any one of their public events – www.erminestreetguard.co.uk has all you need to know.

Ermine Street Guard re-enactment society in action. (© Ermine Street Guard)

While in London, don't miss the very archaeologically centred Museum of London (www.museumoflondon.org.uk). Every region has its share of Roman goodies to put on display though:

☞ In Wales, the National Roman Legionary Museum (www.museumwales.ac.uk/en/roman) houses artefacts from the local ruins of Caerleon fort which was built in AD 75. Caerleon also boasts one of the most complete amphitheatres in Britain and good bath ruins in the centre of town.

☞ The National Museum of Scotland in Edinburgh has a fine collection of Iron Age material and you can see the late Roman silver hoard found at Traprain Law hill-fort.

☞ The Yorkshire Museum in York has many fine Roman finds from the area on display.

☞ Reading Museum and Art Galley has especially strong Roman displays for Silchester.

☞ Corinum Museum in Cirencester has excellent Roman material from sites in both Roman Cirencester and the Cotswolds.

☞ Chester's Newstead Roman Gallery has an impressive collection of Roman tombstones and the story of Roman Chester including models of the *principia* and the amphitheatre (visit the ruins at Little St John Street, near the Roman Gardens). www.grosvenormuseum.co.uk. While in Chester, visit the real Roman (and Saxon and Medieval) ruins beneath Chester at the DEWA Roman Experience with their reconstructions and hands-on approach to history. www.dewaromanexperince.co.uk

☞ Rome has a perennial fascination. Keep an eye open for short-term Roman exhibitions which are regularly on display across the country and especially in London's British Museum (www.britishmuseum.org) which has a fantastic Romano-British gallery and includes the famous very personal Vindolanda tablets.

 ## Reading up

Interest in the Romans is eternal and there is a plethora of books to choose from.

To explore the actual archaeology of Roman Britain further though, find your way around with the Ordnance Survey's *Roman Britain – Historical Map and Guide* (2001). *Roman Britain from the Air* (Cambridge University Press 1983) will give you a new perspective, while a closer look can be gained from Guy de la Bédoyère's *The Finds of Roman Britain* (Batsford 1988) or his more general *Roman Britain: A New History* (Thames & Hudson 2006).

One of English Heritage's contributions to the library of books on Rome is Martin Millett's *Roman Britain* (Batsford/English Heritage 2005) but *Conquest: The Roman*

Invasion of Britain by John Peddie (Tempus Publishing 2005) hones in on the conquest years. The specific topic of forts is studied in David Breeze's *Roman Forts in Britain* (Shire Archaeology 1983) but any number of books can be bought from site shops along Hadrian's Wall. Classic works on the northern frontier are David Breeze and Brian Dobson's *Hadrian's Wall* (Penguin 1997) and Jim Crow's *Housesteads* (Batsford/English Heritage 1995).

Villas are a topic on their own, with books like Peter Johnson's *Romano-British Mosaics* (Shire Archaeology 1982) and David Johnson's *Roman Villas* (Shire Archaeology 1983). Specialist books abound, covering topics such as coins in Roman Britain, amphitheatres here, forts, gods, food and drink, roads, medicine, pottery, towns, brooches ... the list is endless. For life in general, Joan P. Alcock's *Life in Roman Britain* (Tempus Publishing 2006) covers most topics.

If you're short of time though, spin through Peter Salway's *Roman Britain: A Very Short Introduction*, part of Oxford Paperbacks' excellent *Very Short Introduction* series (2000).

Although the Ancient Britons kept no written records, Roman writers used the campaigns in Britain to boost their glory and you can see what they had to say for themselves in Stanley Ireland's *Roman Britain: A Sourcebook* (Routledge second edition 1996). Or you can read all of Julius Caesar's (biased) opinion of Britain in Books IV and V of his *Gallic Wars*. Similarly, Tacitus wrote of his father-in-law's achievements in Britain in *Agricola*. Both are available in English in the Penguin Classics series.

The fate of the doomed Ninth Legion is imaginatively pictured in Rosemary Sutcliff's *The Eagle of the Ninth*. Although a children's fiction book, it has inspired many budding historians.

A dramatic reconstruction of life in Britain towards the end of the Roman occupation can be found in the chapters, *A Centurion of the Thirtieth* and *On the Great Wall*, of Rudyard Kipling's *Puck of Pook's Hill* (published in 1906). Hunt for a copy through internet search engines.

THE DARK AGES

INTRODUCTION: illuminating the darkness

With Rome's central unifying force gone and raiders threatening from all sides, Britain splintered into factions. As the once-proud villas disintegrated into rough, ill-kept hovels and the roads began to fall into disrepair, education slipped and the written word became elusive again. Without grand stone buildings to excavate or a plethora of documents to decipher, archaeologists have comparatively little evidence to enlighten us about the next centuries – it can seem to be limited to a few enigmatic remains of a few post holes here, and a weathered implement or a skeleton there. The so-called Dark Ages had begun.

They stretch from Rome's exit from Britain in AD 410 right up to the Norman Conquest in 1066. Yet, despite their name, these 600 years were certainly not a cultural black hole lacking in life or vibrancy. Admittedly, the early years after the Romans' departure were indeed a time of crumbling decay, as Britain shrank back into smaller rural communities much like those which had met the Romans 400 years previously. These were the misty times of the romantic legends of a post-Roman warrior king called Arthur. Much that had been Roman had gone within a hundred years. But a new culture was being born in its place: the art, houses, clothing, lifestyle and even language of Britain had a new influence now – the Saxon raiders were moving in.

As the great historian of the time, the Venerable Bede, put it, it had all begun when the Britons got together to discuss how they might 'obtain help to repel the frequent fierce attacks of their northern neighbours'. They 'all agreed with the advice of their king, Vortigern, to call on Saxon peoples across the sea.' Thus came Hengest and Horsa, brothers from Jutland in Denmark. But the rescuers liked what they saw, and turned raiders themselves. They seized it by force and stayed. Likewise, the Angles from southern Denmark swarmed into East Anglia and Northern England, the German Saxons flooded into the Thames Valley and Wessex, the Jutes from northern Denmark dominated Kent and the Isle of Wight while the Frisians crossed from northern Holland and the Franks from France and Belgium headed for Kent. It had the air of a general free-for-all.

Even in such fraught times, Britain acquired a new sense of culture. Native Celtic art blended with the new Christian images that came with St Augustine's mission into England in 596/7 and, as monasteries sprang up across the land, literacy prospered within the cloisters. Valuable church plate adorned the altars and rattled in the vestries and the wealth of the monasteries attracted the attentions of the Vikings. They struck Lindisfarne's Holy Island first, in AD 793, and then raided the riches of the Church for many decades. Eventually though they began to settle as well as plunder. Their new Scandinavian place names would become rooted in Northern England's soil while the art and legends of this mixed cosmopolitan population would colour our own concept of story-telling, most markedly seen in J.R.R. Tolkien's work.

Meanwhile, with Rome's absence from the scene, Ireland had been enjoying a second Golden Age. Christianity had arrived here in the fifth century and local kings had encouraged the founding of monasteries, where education and skills in sculpture and metalwork flourished and from where missionaries spread the Word throughout Europe. Being on a route north from the continent, Ireland also imported smart pottery and the literary art of illumination. Their blend of homespun Celtic art mixed with complex designs made the early Irish crosses a powerful inspiration for years to come.

During all this, the Gaelic-speaking Irish, the *Scottii*, had spread into Wales and Cornwall, and had established the Dal Riata kingdom in the west coast of Scotland – eventually absorbing the Celtic *Pictii* ('painted people') who had previously occupied the north and eastern regions and who had been given their derogatory name by the

Romans due to their addiction to tattoos (and out of spite, no doubt, for their ability to remain unconquered by the legions). It was into this kingdom that St Columba arrived from Ireland, brought Christianity in 563 AD and founded the monastery on Iona and spread the Word further afield.

At first, Scotland, Wales and Cornwall remained largely untouched by the Saxon and Angles' incursions and the old traditions thus continued unabated here. Then Angles from Northumberland pushed into southeast Scotland with Edinburgh possibly being named after Edwin, king of Northumberland, in AD 617.

The Vikings struck at the end of the 700s. The Norse and Danish raiders eventually chose to settle down in Shetland and, by the 900s, the north and west coasts and the isles of Scotland were, in effect, provinces of Norway. They served as crucial landing stops on the way to Iceland and the west, including Ireland which was such a favoured destination for raiding and trading that they founded Dublin as a major Viking trading town in the early tenth century.

The Scandinavians had not arrived into an empty chaos in England though. As the first raids terrorised the northern coasts in the last years of the 700s, England was stabilising into four recognised kingdoms: the richest, Northumbria with its capital in York contained a blend of Christian, Celtic and Saxon cultures – its Lindisfarne monastery produced the fabulous illuminated gospels; in East Anglia a seventh-century king had held sway and been buried in style at Sutton Hoo; Mercia had stretched west into Wales until King Offa opted to draw a line with his Offa's Dyke in AD 780. However, by AD 848/899, the Vikings had taken possession of these three kingdoms and the lands east and north of the old Watling Street (running from London to Chester) were now subject to 'Danelaw'. Only Saxon Wessex survived untamed.

Ironically, amidst the centuries of turmoil, Wessex would became the most 'organised' state in Western Europe and it would set the foundations for an enduring (and very English) administration system: when Wessex's King Alfred defeated the Danes in 878 at Guthrum, he went on to develop a defensive system of planned, fortified towns linked by roads just a day's march from each other. Called *burghs*, they were the foundation of our modern 'boroughs'. This decentralised system of order would scatter the population across a multitude of English villages: so much so that most modern English villages owe their once-humble origins to the century that followed.

Even after Alfred died, the dream of freedom from Danelaw lived on: his grandson, Athelstan, was rather wistfully crowned 'King of All Britain' at Kings-ton (Kingston-on-Thames) in 925, but he went on to successfully attack Danelaw in 955. By 973 Alfred's great grandson, Edgar, had a more realistic claim when he was crowned King of England at Bath and Anglo-Saxon magnates and rulers joined in paying him homage.

In those early years of the tenth century the new young king Constantine mac Aed (Constantine II) went on the offensive and united much of what is now modern Scotland into one territory. He renamed the land Alba (which still means 'Scotland' in

Gaelic today), although the apparent stability remained somewhat wobbly with few tenth-century kings going on to rule for more than five years each.

There were signs of cohesion in Wales too as Hywel extended his own rule, codifying existing Welsh laws into the law of Hywel and becoming Hywel Dda ('the Good'). By 1057, his great-great-grandson, Gruffud ap Llywelyn ruled a united, if very rural, Wales.

In the beginning of the Dark Ages there had been chaos and a lack of order. Six hundred years later, our islands had been transformed, through bloodshed, a knack for administration and Christianity, into new kingdoms with new identities. They were lands worth possessing and the Normans now had their eye on them.

◉ LOOK OUT FOR . . .

The Dark Ages are renowned for their lack of archaeological evidence. Despite this, there are actually plenty of features to look out for. The essence is the same as it was for the Romans – settlements, fortifications and religious sites – but the Saxon, Pictish and Viking expression of them was very different.

- ◉ **Anglo-Saxon communities** were rural and timber-built, so there are few traces left for us to find in the landscape. Aerial photos are a boon here – Scotland's Doonhill, off the AI near Dunbar, was once a chieftain's large Anglian hall in the 600s. Yet, despite its scale, it was only spotted by crop marks from the air. Excavated in the 1960s, it is now simply marked out in the grass and explained by a signboard.

- ◉ **Roman villas were re-used** as they fell from splendour: keep a look out at Roman villa sites for the occasional mosaic punctured by a Saxon farmer's hearth or posthole. These showy rooms were now used to house farm animals and even the grand army granaries at Vindolanda were partitioned off, re-cobbled and re-used in the ninth century, long after the Romans had left.

- ◉ **Place names** may not feel like archaeology, but they are just as valuable as a lumpy field is – they point to the origins of settlements. Scan a map instead of tramping the fields and you'll find Danish Viking place names all across Northern England: -by indicates a village (eg. Wetherby, Grimsby and Whitby), -toft a Viking plot of land (Lowestoft), -thorpe a daughter settlement (Scunthorpe and Grimethorpe), –scale a temporary shelter (as in Windscale), and –thwaite a clearing (Yokenthwaite and Braithwaite).

  In the north and west of Scotland the Norwegian Vikings first founded place names with navigational clues in them: the most north-westerly point on the British mainland is Cape Wrath, so named because *hvarf* meant 'turning point', as in 'turn left here boys or you'll end up in L'Anse aux Meadows' (the first Viking colony in Canada). Later, they would use more settled names like *bolstadr* (bister as in Westerbister) for 'farm'.

Even Wales which was never heavily settled by the Vikings has Scandinavian places: Anglesey, Fishguard and the islands of Skomer, Ramsey and Tusker, amongst others, have Viking origins. *Ey* meant 'island' and was often linked to its owner – Anglesey is thought to have derived from 'Ongl's ey', whoever Ongl was.

In comparison, Anglo-Saxon communities were founded with names like *–ham* for a settlement (eg. Caterham, Durham), *–stowe* a meeting place (Felixstowe and Padstow), *-ton* a village (Kingston and Tonbridge), *-wick/h* for a produce (Chiswick produced cheese and Woolwich sheep), or *–stead* as a place (Hampstead and Stanstead).

A list of common place name meanings are helpfully listed on the Domesday Book website ('background' pages), www.domesdaybook. co.uk, and you can search for 'place names glossary' in the OS website, www.ordnancesurvey.co.uk

Viking settlements are hard to recognise in the field – they're rare and varied but it's worth noting that they were always keen on rectangular buildings. They range from the ninth-century farmstead of three rectangular buildings near Ribblehead quarry (on a trail from the B6255) with their 1.5- to 3m-thick rubble-and-packed-earth walls, to the long narrow 'hall houses' and their central hearths flanked by benches at Brough of Birsay on Orkney (check the tide times to reach it by its causeway). An exciting recent discovery in 2008 is the Viking timber-lined cellars found in York's ongoing ground-breaking Hungate Dig which is exploring this vibrant Viking trading town (*colour plate 20*). You can unearth more details on their website, www.dighungate.com

Earthworks and forts provide evidence for the violence of the Dark Ages: hillforts resembling (or even re-using) Iron Age forts were occupied in Scotland's early Dark Ages. Dunadd in Argyll and Bute was the royal centre for the Dal Riata kingdom. Situated on a craggy hilltop that had been occupied in the Iron Age, a strange Pictish-style boar has been inscribed which helps to date its ruined walls, although a carved bowl and foot imprint remain a possible, if mysterious, link to the old rituals of

TOP TIP

Beware the Camelot / King Arthur connection claims that you will encounter at any number of forts. He may well have been real, but his legend has been interwoven with myth and fictional strands from Victorian romance.

kingship and connections with the earth. A very late Ogham inscription (dated to between the eighth and tenth centuries) implies the site was still in use after the Vikings moved into Scotland.

Many sizeable linear earthworks (like Offa's Dyke) were built as boundaries but their styles vary which makes them notoriously tough to date – comparison with other local features is often our only clue. For example, if they cut through Roman features they must be later than the Roman era – like the parallel banks paired with outer ditches which can be seen from the modern road between Grinton and Fremington in Swaledale. But, because the ditches are ignored by Fremington's known pre-medieval features, they probably predate them: hence the fifth- to seventh-century estimate for their construction.

Single farmsteads have always been the norm but, in Dark Age Ireland, clusters of timber and mud-based roundhouses and outbuildings were huddled together for mutual protection from raiders. Protected by circular earthwork ramparts, there were literally thousands of these 'ringforts' or 'raths'. The larger ones are difficult to distinguish from Iron Age fort ramparts but if you find a souterrain in an Irish fort, you're probably looking at an early Christian site.

Irish souterrains, unlike the earlier English and Scottish underground stores which date from the late Iron Age, are usually post-Christian. Marked as 'caves' on the OS maps, their construction varies widely, some being of heavy stones, others being cut into clay or rock. They squirm round bends and revel in narrowing traps, blind tunnels and concealed passages to trap the unwary raider like some homespun *Indiana Jones* adventure – these were clearly desperate means to hide yourself, your food or your riches from raiders.

◉ **Ogham inscriptions** originated in Ireland and were used between the third and sixth centuries in areas of Irish settlement, ie. in Ireland, north and west Scotland and Wales. They're identifiable as rows of lines etched on the edges of stones – check the edges of Pictish stones and stone pillars in or around souterrains and for them.

Ogham inscribed stone set into the windowsill of St Brynach's Parish church in Nevern, Wales. (© Janis Heward)

👁 **The advent of Christianity** brought new features into the land: Saxon Churches were often demolished by the later Normans and therefore few have survived. Those that have are little more than small, simple aisle-less naves: Greenstead church (Essex) even had no windows. When there were windows, they were small and splayed out to both the exterior and interior. Austere Anglo-Saxon stone churches with fine square towers appeared for defensive reasons after the 899 Danelaw split – like those at St Peter's (Barton-on-Humber), Rothwell (Lincs) and Bosham (Sussex). Central columns gradually appeared. The outside of St Lawrence at Bradford-on-Avon is decorated with typical Saxon external blind arcading, tapered arches and doorways and two carved angels.

A lack of a church didn't deter the early Christians. Preaching (or high) crosses were erected to mark open-air worship sites. Pagan mythology and Christian imagery lived, literally, side by side on these crosses as Scandinavian, Celtic and Saxon art were all fused together in the art of Britain's early Christian monuments. The stylistic development of these crosses went roughly like this:

☞ **AD 400s/early 500s:** The earliest Christian memorial stones were inscribed with Latin and Christian symbols such as the cross or the chi-rho. The earliest known are in a church porch in Kirkmadrine, Galloway. Irish crosses of the time can include the Ogham script.

☞ **AD 600s:** Simple but large stone crosses were carved with names.

☞ **Early 700s:** Latin was still used but religious scenes are combined with leafy vines, animal tracery and Saxon runes (the runes on Ruthwell Cross in Dumfries and Galloway quote an Old English poem, The Dream of the Rood).

☞ **AD 700s:** Pagan stone circles were re-used and 'purified' by simple and sometimes multiple carvings of crosses (e.g. Laggangairn standing stones).

☞ **Late 700s-800s:** Iona Crosses (the 'Celtic cross' design) carried an eternal circle around the head of the cross but carvings of stylised vines were still continuing.

The base of tenth-century Penmon cross in Anglesey. (© Gillian Hovell)

☞ **AD 900s-1000s:** fine geometric designs on crosses echoed metalwork design of the time, and interlaced tailed dragon-like beasts and simpler plait designs featured on high crosses. Kilmorie's stone (near Stranraer) includes Thor's hammer, tongs and eagles in this typical tenth-century mix.

As Christian crosses were being erected, the Picts were developing their own style of carved stones. They are now categorized into three 'classes':

☞ **Class I:** These early sixth- to eighth-century designs on unworked stones are enigmatic, involving a serpent, Z-shaped rod, double-disc, mirror and comb and some animals – but absolutely no crosses (*colour plate 21*).

☞ **Class II:** Dating mostly from the eighth and ninth centuries these are mostly rectangular with a large cross stuffed full of busy designs carved in relief on one side (looking remarkably like manuscript illumination patterns of the time). The reverse contains a crowded scene, often with Pictish symbols and even Ogham script (*colour plate 22*).

☞ **Class III:** These first appear in the eighth or ninth century and have no Pictish symbols but can be full of figures recording some event. They are cross-slabs (i.e. slabs with crosses carved on them), free-standing crosses or just recumbent grave markers (decorated with crosses). Unique to Britain are the Anglo-Viking hogbacks which can be found in southern Scotland and northern England. These stone grave markers of the tenth to twelfth centuries have curved backs which represent the roof of a house – Govan in Glasgow has some good examples.

The monastic settlements of the Dark Ages were numerous but small. The Irish sites include ruins of one or more churches (it was easier to rebuild than repair or extend them) but most refectories, workshops and guesthouses were timber and have long gone. A few were stone based, with projecting antae (stone pillars which were integral to the doorway) but nearly every monastery has been overbuilt by later early medieval stone structures.

Seventh-century monastic crypts sometimes survive, lurking beneath later churches – Ripon, Sudbury and Hexham all hide these 1300 year-old secrets in arched tunnels reached by steep stone steps. Relics were once kept in these dimly lit passages.

Where to go

Substantial remains from the Dark Ages are few and far between. No 'Stonehenges' here – just a tantalizing collection of subtle but important clues into the hazy days of the Saxon kings and Scandinavian raiders and settlers.

Map of Britain: Dark Age sites.
(© Andrew Hovell)

Finnis, Co. Down

1   Irish souterrains date from these Dark Ages and they litter the country. At Finnis in Co. Down one runs underground for around 29m with two shorter side passages. Dating from around the ninth century, its drystone walling is now lit by solar power (but a torch still helps!).

Ogham stones

2   The carved lines of Ogham Script were used wherever the Dark Age Irish settled. Hundreds of 'ogham stones' exist in Ireland – Stone Craig in Co. Tyrone is just one of them. They were sometimes reused as capping stone in souterrains (which all helps to date the souterrains as later than the ogham script years). Ogham appears on some Pictish stones, such as the Class II stone, now housed in the ruined Chapel of St Fergus Kirk near Dyce (Aberdeen) airport.

Tayside and Grampian

3   All three classes of Pictish stones can be seen in the Pictish heartlands of Tayside and Grampian.

Class III Pictish Stone at St Vigean's church.
(© Janis Heward)

- *Eight mysterious Class I stones* can be viewed in Inverness museum and one of the stones by the roadside in Aberlemno (Angus) is a beautiful example.
- *The cross-and-busily-designed Class II stones* include the extraordinary must-see 6.5m/20ft high Sueno Stone outside Forres. The smaller Maiden Stone in Grampian is a more usual example.
- *Two excellent Class III stones/crosses* are also in Aberlemno in Tayside.
- *Several stones of every class* can be seen in the Museum of Scotland in Edinburgh.
- *To see over twenty Pictish stones* in one place head for Meigle Sculptured Stone Museum in Perthshire, and Groam Museum in Rosemarkie on the Black Isle has a good range too.

Gosforth, Cumbria

4 One of the most fascinating high stone crosses is at Gosforth in Cumbria. Three metres tall, it is carved with a panoply of Norse gods blended with Christianity. The crucified Christ is triumphant, lording it above the evil god, Loth who is chained beneath a snake and Woden who fights a wolf surrounded by dragons.

Whithorn and Dumfries and Galloway

5 The progression of cross styles can be followed on a number of crosses in Whithorn and Dumfries and Galloway especially.

Bishop Auckland

6 The restored Escomb Saxon church near Bishop Auckland in Co. Durham is one of the finest examples of early Christian architecture in Northern Europe. It was built in around AD 670 using stone salvaged from the nearby Roman fort of Binchester and retains its seventh-century early shape and style. With three stone crosses to view, a rare Anglo-Saxon serpent-decorated sundial still in situ in the south wall and, two square headed splayed windows and the simple Celtic door in the north wall, there is much to see here.

Escomb Saxon church is well worth a visit.
(© Janis Heward)

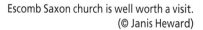

Sutton Hoo

7 The great treasures found in seventh-century princely burials at Sutton Hoo (and nearby Taplow) in Suffolk remind us that this was a time of great craftsmanship and trade as the gold, silver, bronze, iron, wood, leather, enamelled and jewelled riches came from as far as Sweden and Egypt. Visit the mounds themselves and the exhibition's full-size reconstruction of the burial chamber. However, to see the famous helmet and many original finds, you have to go to the British Museum in London.

Offa's Dyke

8 At 270km (140 miles) long, Offa's Dyke runs roughly along the modern border between England and Wales. Built between AD 757 and 796 its 4m (12ft) ditch and rampart were over 20m wide and 8m high in total and topped by a wooden palisade and manned watch-towers (but no large gateways). Worn down by time, farming and development, you now have to pick your vantage spot with care (try the section near Edenhope Hill in Shropshire or Tintern's Devil's Pulpit's viewpoint) but a healthy long-distance walk runs its length.

Scottish forts

9 The tumbled walls of massive ramparts are reminiscent of Iron Age forts and, to be fair, several Iron Age forts were reused in the Dark Ages (like Whithorn's promontory fort) as they provided good pre-prepared defensive ground. Carvings give the age away – a Z-shape, abstract animals and human heads are typical Pictish carvings and can be found on the lumpy hill called the Mark of Mote in south Dumfries and Galloway. Class I Pictish carvings of bulls were found on the outer walls of the central fort at Burghead in Moray. This is the largest Pictish fort in Scotland and it was a powerful naval base at the time – you can still see its huge ramparts.

Shetland

10 Jarlshof in Shetland was home to Vikings between the eighth and twelfth centuries – a rare extensive set of farm building foundations can still be seen at the west end of this major site, including those of a stone-and-turf two-roomed

20m x 7m longhouse, a smithy, a barn and a burnt-stone sauna. Judging by the finds discovered here, these Vikings were farmers and fishermen, not warriors, thereby backing up the *Orkeyinga Saga*'s report of a peaceful community that lived here in the twelfth century.

You also get to see a community of small Bronze Age houses (similar to Skara Brae's), a bronze smith's site (c.800 BC) and related middens all at the eastern end. To the south

Jarlshof on Shetland is a site packed with features (© Liz Forrest)

1 Excavations like these at the fort at Vindolanda may be the immediate image of archaeology that comes to mind but there is far more to archaeology than digging. (© The Vindolanda Trust)

2 Fountains Abbey in Yorkshire. Heritage sites are among our most popular leisure attractions. (© Gillian Hovell)

3 Ancient wall remains on open moorland. (© Gillian Hovell)

4 Callanish Stones. (© Liz Forrest)

5 Discarded burnt stones like these were heaped in mounds around water-boilers. (© Gillian Hovell)

6 Pentre Ifan, Pembrokeshire

7 Isbister's 'Tomb of the Eagles' and its unique trolley entrance. (© Andrew Hovell)

8 A few stones in a line, sticking out of the heather like broken teeth, may be all that remains of a prehistoric boundary. (© Gillian Hovell)

9 Mam Tor's steep ramparts are impressive even in the mist. They surround a dramatic hill that is topped by two Bronze Age burial mounds. (© Gillian Hovell)

10 The Great Orme Copper Mines. (© Gillian Hovell)

Left: 11 A reconstruction Bronze Age workshop at Archaeolink Prehistory Park. (© supplied by Archaeolink Prehistory Park)

Below left: 12 The remains of roundhouses can be as elusive as this roughly circular platform edged by a battered ridge. (© Gillian Hovell)

Right: 13 The structure of the cavity wall at Glenelg is clearly visible. (© Liz Forrest)

Below: 14 The Scottish Crannog Centre brings these remarkable island homes to life. (© Liz Forrest)

15 An Iron Age roundhouse under construction at Butser's experimental farm. (© Helen Hovell)

16 The murals that survive at Dover's Painted House reveal the grandeur of Roman wall paintings: this was no ordinary wallpaper. (© Brian Philp, Kent Archaeological Rescue Unit)

17 At Fishbourne Palace an old mosaic can be seen beneath the damaged, newer design. (© Andrew Hovell)

18 The iconic image of Hadrian's Wall, looking east towards Housesteads Fort. (© Gillian Hovell)

19 Dover Painted House is the place to go for wall paintings in Britain. (© Brian Philp, Kent Archaeological Rescue Unit)

20 Viking Age timber-lined Cellar, unearthed at Hungate Dig in York, 2008. (© Yorkshire Archaeological Trust's Hungate Dig)

21 Symbolic carvings on a Class I Pictish Stone at Aberlemno, Angus (© Janis Heward)

22 A cross decorates the front of this Class II Pictish Stone at Aberlemo but figures galore and Pictish symbols fill the back. (© Janis Heward)

23 Viking re-enactments are to live and die for (© Andrew Horeckyj, Vikings! of Middle England)

24 Pack horses are still in action today – these ones carry loads in and out of the Grand Canyon in Arizona, USA. (© Gillian Hovell)

25 Platforms of bright green grass may be old charcoal clamps. (© Gillian Hovell)

26 The nightmarish 'Ladder of Salvation' mural. (Reproduced with permission from Chaldon church)

27 Reconstructed late medieval hall at Weald and Downland Open Air Museum. Note the lack of chimney and open hearth. (Reproduced with permission of Weald and Downland Open Air Museum)

28 Oriel window at the Archbishop's Palace in Croydon (now the Old Palace of John Whitgift School). (© Liz Forrest)

29 A typical 'doughnut' of spoil around a disused mine shaft. (© Gillian Hovell)

30 Bembridge pill box as it was before it was incorporated into the sea defences. (© Andrew Hovell)

31 The world's first iron bridge towers 45ft above the Ironbridge Gorge (© Andrew Hovell)

32 Weather brewing over Dartmoor stone circle. (© Andrew Hovell)

are stunning Iron Age wheelhouses and a Pictish earthhouse and two medieval farm buildings share the site, as do the ruins of an early seventeenth-century laird's house. All in all, a great place to practice your archaeological dating skills!

Abernethy

11 A rare feature that's worth discovering for yourself if you don't suffer from vertigo is the Scottish Round Tower: only two of these windowless Irish-style monastic refuges-cum -watchtowers built in c.1000 AD survive. Abernethy's is a stunning 74ft high with a broken Pictish stone at its base and, although its original wooden floors and ladders have long gone, you can climb a metal spiral staircase to its top. The other is at Brechin (also in Tayside) and is attached to the cathedral there.

What was life like?

A common image of the Dark Ages is that of Saxon and Viking raiders raping and pillaging helpless timber villages while hooded monks flee, clutching their holy books and the church silver. There can be no denying the violence of the time: the Iron Age style forts, ramparts and hidden souterrains of the early Dark Ages bear witness to it. So do the chronicles of the time – *The Ruin of Britain*, written by the fifth-century monk, Gildas, and the *Anglo-Saxon Chronicles* (yearly accounts of major events) depict a world gripped by chaos and horror (*colour plate 23*).

Nearly a hundred years on, whole communities were still being mercilessly slaughtered – even the old Roman fort at Pevensey, recommissioned as defences against the raiders, failed to protect the trembling locals from invading Saxons.

In time, the raiders settled and became part of the native population. The seventh-century warrior princes of the land were being buried with showy Anglo-Saxon helmets and swords, the style of which are celebrated even today in modern films like *The Lord of the Rings*. The Old English poetry celebrates both this macho culture and the role of *wifmen* who were buried with their spindles and 'weaving' (the origin of *wif*) tools – yet the documents that have survived show that Anglo-Saxon women had equal rights to inherit and bequeath and clearly owned property in their own right. A warrior culture it may have been, but it's worth noting that, in Pictish lands, it was matri-linear succession that gave rulers their authority.

The raiders had arrived in a land without much centralised control – family and tribal ties were what mattered – and they lived a rural life that was completely tied to the seasons' produce. For centuries, each year was played out with a repeated pattern of alternating feast and famine. Indeed, Lenten fasting would have its benefits, providing as it did a much-needed spiritual side to the sparseness of dwindling winter reserves. When atrocious weather at the end of the tenth century caused crops to rot in the fields and a 'great pestilence among cattle' destroyed whole herds the desperate apparently resorted to suicide and the accepted practice of infanticide was deemed a necessary act of survival.

The *Julian Work Calendar* of 1020 shows scrawny and rugged labourers, bound as they were to work the land for their lords as virtual slaves, all toiling on the land as they ploughed with a team of eight small oxen or tended their sheep – and the archaeology of bones (osteo-archaeology) gives us painful confirmation of swollen joints and whole lives spent in hard physical labour.

But the rich ate well, taking the produce from the poor's labour. If it was edible, it would be eaten: fat-free free-range pigs, cattle, sheep and chicken were to hand but game birds and venison were hunted too. No fish went to waste: pike, minnows, lampreys and eels joined trout and salmon on the table, along with herrings, oysters and cockles. The monks in the abbeys were forbidden four-legged, red blooded meat so they swapped grafts and clippings of fruit trees, grew vegetables and ate chicken, while dodgily, but conveniently, classing anything (regardless of how many legs it had) that lived in or on the water as 'fish'– and traces of the numerous fishponds they created can still be found in the land. Bee hives were a valuable asset too, providing honey, the only sweetener of the time, and a healing balm, as well as beeswax for candles which gave a steady light with a pleasant smell instead of the regular pong from tallow candles made from mutton fat.

Meanwhile, however, Ireland was thriving and producing a complex multi-cultural blend of art in stone crosses, church silver (Ardagh Chalice stands out) and illuminated manuscripts. After Columba brought Christianity to Iona in 565, both monasteries and nunneries sprouted around the northern lands. Abbess Hilda founded the Abbey of Whitby (on the Yorkshire coast) where both monks and nuns lived a rare exemplary life and it was here, at the Synod of Whitby in 664, that the ever-contentious date of Easter was settled. It was here too that King Oswy of Northumbria listened to delegates from the Celtic and Roman churches to decide which rule England should follow. In the end, it was the Roman tradition established in Canterbury by Augustine in 597 who won the right to stamp their mark on British Christianity.

Monasteries such as Bede's Jarrow and Lindisfarne would go on to be responsible for a kind of mini renaissance of literacy and art – the Lindisfarne's gospels are still one of our greatest national treasures and are a 'must-see' in London's British Library. But literacy was the privilege of the church. Out in the fields, Ireland was already using its own Ogham alphabet of lines inscribed down the edges of stones while in England runes began to be scratched on anything from tombs to weapons and combs. Associated with magical properties, they were used mostly from the fifth century and largely in the south and east of England. Saxon settlers used a version of Germanic runes while the Scandinavians brought their own *futharks* runes (some of which were scratched as Viking graffiti inside Maes Howe's ancient burial chamber). Wales, however, enjoyed its own dawning of a literary age as the earliest Welsh language literature was written even as the Anglians eyed the mountains – the magnificent Heledd poems bewail the pain of the advance on Powys.

The tattered remains of Latin were ousted from everywhere but the internationally linked church, and in England it was replaced with the settlers' earthy Germanic Old

English. The Anglo-Saxon rural way of life planted our farming vocabulary firmly into our heritage: ground, earth and ox are all theirs.

These settlers preferred timber buildings to the cold stone of Rome. However, it was the Vikings who created the first real towns seen since the Romans. They made trading centres like *Jorvik* (York) their own. Urban life was regenerated and a thriving river and coastal trade flourished; Chinese silk, Red Sea cowrie shells and Baltic amber were on the shopping list, while ivory, glass and jet sold alongside the familiar pottery, metal, wood, wool, leather, stone and bone goods. Livings were made from specific trades – the beginnings perhaps of a culture where guilds would arise in future times. Hard silver hand-struck currency regulated their sales and carried both pagan and Christian symbols side by side, so that Scandinavian paganism and Christianity rubbed shoulders in life as well as on the high crosses found in regions as diverse as Lincolnshire's Halton and Yorkshire's Middleton.

If towns were making a comeback, the once-Roman reliance on prayers for cures had never really left. Books such as the ninth-century *Bald's Leechbook* invoked both God and holy items as cures for tumours, lunacy and even women's gossip. The small Saxon churches often housed a saint's relics which, it was claimed, performed miraculous cures. Such prized bones and splinters of crosses drew pilgrims, and therefore money, to the church. It was here that the horrors of Dark Ages justice were carried out: trial by ordeal decided the guilt or innocence of those accused of crimes ranging from theft to witchcraft and from incest to murder. Within the holy space of the church, the accused would carry a red hot bar for nine paces: if you were healing after three days you were pure, but festering flesh meant a festering heart of sin, and punishment was usually a fine, calculated on a sliding scale depending on how important the person sinned against was. The resulting debt and even slavery were not uncommon (the largest slave market in eleventh-century western Europe operated in nearby Dublin). Death penalties were rarer but the local gallows were a familiar dark shape on the horizon. Naturally (for the time) some criminals were more equal than others: the rich could bail themselves out of their dues. But as the Dark Ages flickered in their final years, King Ethelred ordered in AD 997 that law should be dispensed by the Shire Reeve (sheriff) and twelve good men who were sworn in – and the first twitchings of trial by jury was beginning.

Life was clearly insecure though. At the turn of the millennium, King Ethelred the Unready's counsellors advised that the only way to keep a fresh wave of Scandinavian pirates at bay was to cough up and pay the Danegold. This protection money kept the dozens of local Anglo-Saxon mints busy stamping out coins, some of which have now resurfaced after 1000 years of being buried in a hoard – were they hidden for safe keeping, or maybe the hoards were a response to the reported myth that a Viking could take any treasure to the afterlife if he buried it while he was still alive?

By 1000 AD, Britain was still a largely rural society, although vibrant trading towns now existed and some hints of law and order, albeit rather roughly, had returned. But who could have known that within a single generation that ragged law and order was going to be enforced by a very sudden, very firm, and very Norman, fist?

Things to do

The Dark Ages exude mystery and legend. Their art weaves stories of mythical times and words like 'hordes' and 'rape' and 'pillage' rush from historians' pens. But how can we get a more focused view of life in these misty ages?

Hands-on archaeology lets you in at the sharp end of a trowel. The Hungate Dig in York is a sister site to Jorvik and gives you the opportunity to join in the excavations and experience a personal encounter with the Viking world (and Medieval and Victorian ones too). There's nothing quite like handling the dirt and artefacts yourself to dispel the myths of clichéd history – this is history for real. Here the daily world of the Vikings is coming to life before our eyes. If you don't want to dig, you can tour the ongoing excavations for a wonderfully small fee.

With few written records to guide our understanding of the Dark Ages, the analysis of skeletons from this time is a crucial piece in the jigsaw of archaeological clues. The largest historic bone resource in Britain is based around the 1000 year-old St Peter's church in Barton-upon-Humber. Here, nearly 3000 burials dating from the Anglo-Saxon period up to the Victorian era have been examined in this ambitious project. The church itself happens to have a complete Anglo-Saxon tower and rare baptistry from c.970, making it a great Dark Age site in itself. But the *Buried Lives* interactive exhibition includes reconstructed skeletons and shows us more than just the bare bones of what skeletal remains can tell us.

To see how the Anglo-Saxons lived rather than died visit West Stow Saxon village in Suffolk. It was inhabited from about AD 420 to 650 and, because the houses were all timber-based, there would be little to see here now other than a few linear lumps in the ground except that this site has been reconstructed on its original foundations. Researched from the archaeology found here and similar sites across northern Europe, the buildings in this grand experimental archaeology project include the Great Hall and houses built over a floorboarded shallow pit – go into the houses and experience early Anglo-Saxon life, complete with pigs and chickens. The visitor centre here is home to the majority of the borough's archaeology collections and takes you through Suffolk's history from earliest man to the end of the medieval times.

Another recreated Anglo-Saxon demonstration farm with its timber buildings and farm animals gives vitality to the excavated artefacts and its celebration of the life of the Venerable Bede and the time he lived in. *Bede's World* is located next door to

St Paul's monastery in Jarrow in Northumbria and has events throughout the year. See www.bedesworld.co.uk

A major display of over 900 treasures can be seen in the new Anglo-Saxon and Viking gallery at Norwich Castle Museum and Art

Taking part in Hungate Dig, York. (Reproduced with permission of Hungate Dig)

gallery. Designated by the government as 'outstanding' the gallery includes plenty of interactive activities, including the opportunity to listen to some Old English poetry. Go to www.museums.norfolk.gov.uk

Shatter your illusions of cultural poverty in the Dark Ages by visiting the Lindisfarne Gospels at the British Library and the Sutton Hoo treasures which are ranked among the British Museum's Top Ten Treasures, along with the seventh-century Taplow finds.

A more stomach-churning trip into the past is available at Jorvik, the world famous visitor centre in the heart of modern York. It takes you on a journey in time and physically carries you through the reconstructed (and very smelly) Viking streets of a tenth-century Jorvik town – all based on evidence from the Coppergate digs of 1979-81 when 40,000 artefacts were uncovered and 8 tonnes of soil were shifted. Exhibitions and face-to-face meetings with a Viking complete the experience. York is the venue for an annual Viking festival – walk the streets and watch hundreds of Viking warriors, bards, craftsmen and women strut their stuff and sell their wares. www.yorkfestivals.com will give you the dates.

Vikingar! in Ayrshire is a multi-media award-winning attraction that centres on the Vikings in Scotland. A film and costumed guides and story-tellers take you through 500 years of history, show you a longhouse and introduce you to the Viking gods.

Vikings! Of Middle England are a re-enactment group based in Leicester who provide dynamic events that seek to shock, scare, amuse and educate audiences – check out their website, www.vikingsofmiddleengland.co.uk for their diary of displays or join them yourself for an historically accurate taste of life and death at the sharp end of a Viking sword.

For a Christian landscape experience, visit Whithorn Island, the cradle of Christianity in Scotland with a traditional date of AD 397 for St. Ninian's work. Its museum is stuffed full of finds, grave markers and crosses from the chapels and you can see the stone foundations of the humble, single-entranced, one-roomed Chapel Finian at Mochrum which served pilgrims en route to St. Ninian's shrine at Barhobble on the island.

Lastly, for a truly spiritual as well as archaeological encounter with early Christianity, Iona, off the Isle of Mull is a must.

Reading up

Background reading for the Dark Ages includes several books by television historians, including *Britain AD: A Quest for Arthur, England and the Anglo-Saxons* by Francis Pryor (HarperCollins Publisher Ltd) and *In Search of the Dark Ages* Michael Wood (BBC Books 2005) on the years between the Romans and the Norman Conquest of 1066.

The Year 1000: What Life was like at the Turn of the First Millennium by Robert Lacey is a highly entertaining guide to daily life a thousand years ago.

If you want a quick guide to the Dark Ages, two very readable contributions in the *Very Short Introduction* series by Oxford Paperbacks are *The Anglo-Saxon Age: A Very*

Short Introduction by John Blair (2000) and *The Vikings: A Very Short Introduction* by television historian, Julian D. Richards (2005).

Special interest books are available on the battles of the Dark Ages, Dark Age origins of towns and trade, magic and mystery in the Dark Ages. Books exist on Saxon topics as varied as weapons and warfare, Old English, clothing, the church, food, coins, manuscripts and more.

Get a feel for the turmoil of the time by reading the contemporary *The Anglo-Saxon Chronicles* and Bede's *Ecclesiastical History of the English People* (several versions of each, with various translators and editors are available). Enter a Viking world of battles, sorcery and political murders in the *Orkneyinga Saga*, translated by Hermann Palsson and Paul Edwards (Penguin Classics 1978).

THE MEDIEVAL AGES

INTRODUCTION

In 1064, Edward the Confessor was on the throne of England and Harold Godwinson was angling to be the next king. But, during a diplomatic visit to Normandy, Harold was tricked into swearing over a saint's bones that the English throne would go to William, Duke of Normandy. When Edward died two years later in 1066, England tottered on the verge of events that were to change the British way of life – and its landscape – for ever.

When William won the day and the crown at the Battle of Hastings, not only would all the high offices of the land soon belong to the Normans, but the countryside would become dominated by towering castles raised up on man-made hills and new stone churches with brand new architectural styles would smash aside the Saxon churches.

Norman values would reach right up into Scotland – when Malcolm III's first wife died around 1069, he married a Saxon, Margaret. When Malcolm died their sons took refuge in the English court. Their youngest son, David, spent most of his adolescence there, soaking up the Norman ways before being enthroned as King David I of Scotland in 1124. He became one of the great kings of Scotland. He installed his Norman friends in Scottish lands and, with their help, his abbeys and stone castles with their powerful central towers ('keeps') would spread across the country. Henry II of England, on the other hand, would soon become *the* great castle keep builder. The remains of many of his finest keeps can still be seen today. Over the centuries, castles grew in size and complexity, developing new features according to the needs of their day.

Wales, meanwhile, had collapsed into separate feuding lordships following Gruffudd ap Llewellyn's fall in 1063. Each one vigorously protected their lands against the Normans. At the end of the 1200s though, Edward I began his equally vigorous campaigns to conquer both Wales and Scotland. His vengeful attacks on Scotland would fire up the Scottish Wars of Independence (1296-1362). On both side of the border lands, houses of the rich and poor alike were upgraded to mini-castles – for now, an Englishman's home (and a Scot's home, come to that) was literally, his castle.

In the late thirteenth and fourteenth centuries, Norman castles spread into Ireland and, taking advantage of strategic sites (as well as making a painful cultural point), were even built on ancient forts and burial mounds.

The fourteenth century ripped the heart out of Britain: not only was the Hundred Years War with France heavily taxing Britain but years of appalling weather were devastating crops and disease was striking down livestock. Those who survived starvation were then struck by the plague in 1348 and the years following. As the country reeled, society was, often literally, in ruins as empty houses were left to crumble. When the plague finally released its grip, it was clear that things would never be the same again. With a drastically reduced workforce, the common tenant-cum-land worker was, for the first time, a valuable asset and could insist on fairer wages or head into town to earn a living – those who previously had no opportunities in life now had new doors opened to them (just as women worked in the twentieth century in the manpower-starved days of the First World War). As economic pressure emptied the villages, the buildings were left to decay until nothing remained except scars in the ground.

The medieval ways changed beyond all recognition: wars, plagues and new ideas had been catalysts for great social change. The archaeology we find in the later medieval age reflects this: castles and fortified houses were giving way to domestic displays of wealth by a new class of landed gentry; guildhalls in the now flourishing towns provided career security, a sense of community for the new skilled tradesmen who flocked in from the country, and a solace that the Church had failed to do during the plague; and the new technology of gunpowder had prompted the urgent building of artillery forts.

When Henry VII took the throne of England, Wales and Ireland after the Battle of Bosworth in 1485 he founded the Tudor dynasty. By then, almost all that remained of the early medieval days was the monasteries. Founded amidst oaths of poverty 400 years previously, they had spent centuries gaining land and wealth until they now rivalled the King's power. Vast areas of Britain owed their appearance and their way of life to the monks' enterprising grip on the land – but Henry VIII was about to change that forever and the Tudors would transform Britain into a new land with a new way of life.

TOP TIP

The Normans were originally Norsemen who had been allowed to settle in a region in Northern France. The French ruler, Charles the Simple (son of King Louis the Stammerer and nephew of Charles the Fat) hoped they and their leader, Rollo, would protect the area from future Viking raids. Little did he know that their efficiency in administration and proficiency in war would make them a dominant power in western Europe.

The grand remains from the medieval ages are the castles, monasteries and churches. But the effects of hundreds of years of medieval land management, industry and housing have left their mark too.

⊚ **Deserted medieval villages** are marked on OS maps. They were abandoned due to the plague, climate change and/or economic forces. Visit them when the sun is low on a winter's morning or late afternoon and use your imagination to rebuild houses, enclosures, roads and even churches from the silent grassy platforms and lumps and bumps.

⊚ **Deer leaps.** Hunting was the past-time of the Norman rich and traces of their deer parks survive today. Royal permission granted the construction of 'deer leaps' where a combination of an outer bank and a steep inner bank allowed deer to enter the park but prevented them from leaping out again – thus providing free fresh game for the lords.

⊚ **The major fuel of the time was charcoal**. It was clean, smokeless and a renewable resource. Trees were carefully managed by coppicing (cutting the trunk so they grow multiple new stems from the wound). This provided the ideal raw material for charcoal – fresh inch-thick shoots of growth every year. It also prolonged the tree's life and veteran trees which were planted in the medieval times still stand today. Look for wide knobbly bases, from which thick multiple trunks have grown.

600-year-old alder tree, planted in medieval days. (© Gillian Hovell)

⊚ **Medieval fields** were small and the regular plough team of eight small oxen resulted in S-shaped fields being easier to plough but there were many long, thin fields too. Broken lines of trees dotted across large modern fields or a low stony, much grassed-over mound are often all that remains of old hedgerows or boundaries of the smaller fields. Some old fields can still be spotted by their shape on OS maps but don't forget to look for field shapes on old historic maps too.

⊚ **Examples of medieval ridge and furrow marks** can be found across much of the Midlands of England and beyond, but they are rare as they only survive if a field has been left largely unploughed since the medieval times. Low sunlight and a smattering of snow can highlight the striped corrugated appearance of these fields. Aerial photographs sometimes show them up too. The higher ridges seem to have been self-draining seedbeds and the low furrows a drain – or maybe they were an insurance policy: a dry summer favoured growth in the furrow while in a wet summer the ridge crops would flourish. Beware: especially wide ridges in a field framed by an encircling furrow, or narrow (2–3m) ridges, are probably a produce of later nineteenth-century steam ploughing.

- 👁 **Trade routes**. It's a popular misconception that no-one travelled much in the past. Trade routes flourished and produce was carried for miles on efficient 'trains' of multiple packhorses – the juggernauts of their day (*colour plate 24*). Rivers were spanned by specially-constructed packhorse bridges: narrow with one high arch spanning the river, they had low edges so that the pannier loads didn't snag on the walls. Notice though that most medieval stone bridges were built after 1300 and were only about 3 or 4m wide, requiring triangular projections on them to allow pedestrians to step back when wheeled traffic was crossing.

- 👁 **Tithe barns** were a regular part of medieval life, providing storage for the taxed 'tenth' of produce that went to the church. Few survive but tiny slot windows for ventilation, a high double-doored entrance and a steep (once thatched) roof with gable ends are the hallmarks of these buildings.

Medieval industry was localised, which means that there are signs of it just about everywhere:

- 👁 **Large circles of bright green grass** in rough fields may be the site of charcoal clamps where the wood was transformed into fuel – over the centuries the ashes have acted as fertiliser improving the grass (*colour plate 25*). Beware though: these platforms can be caused by modern circular cattle feeders levelling the ground! Rabbits love burrowing in the loose soil of the clamps – kick through the soil they scratch out to see if there's any tell-tale charcoal in it.

- 👁 **Watermills** were the powerhouses of their day and were used to grind grain, hammer iron and treat cloth (fulling). Mentioned as valuable assets in the Domesday Book, there were thousands of them but, because the mill itself was made of timber, all that survives now are usually just the silted-up channels (leats or goits) and clay-lined ponds which supplied water to the mill from a river or stream.

- 👁 **Bloomery furnaces** are a specialist's feature and are little explored by archaeologists but they lurk in unimproved fields everywhere. Their ruined and levelled-off remains are often simply a shallow hollow, roughly 1m across, edged by a grassed-over, horseshoe of crumbling stones revetted into the ground behind it. Every village had a blacksmith, and it seems likely that just about any area with access to iron ore had at least one iron smelting site, so keep a look out in rough, unimproved fields.

On the domestic front ...

👁 **Houses** which have survived from the medieval period have often all but vanished under later additions and adaptations. However, there are several distinctive medieval features you can look out for.

The simplest houses were cruck buildings, made from a series of pairs of curving timbers which met at the top – look for protruding flat stones (padstones) which supported the beams at the corners of the (rare) surviving longhouses (now often rebuilt in stone). The poor lived in one room and their animals were housed in the second room whose floor often sloped to drain the muck away from the living area.

In the late medieval times, the richest built the first brick houses and, with the advent of chimneys, they could now tile their roofs instead of using thatch which had filtered the smoke. Multiple chimneys soon became a mark of status and wealth. Glass appeared in windows too.

For the slightly less rich, a half-way house, so to speak, was the half-timbered style (often referred to as 'Tudor') with white plaster between the dark timbers that patterned the external walls.

👁 **Castles.** The Normans' very first impact on our landscape was their timber-kit castles but they were soon replacing them with stone ones. The earliest Scottish stone castles (Tioram, Dunstaffnage, Mingary and Sween) were built from the late 1100s. Their designs changed over the centuries and, as a result, we can still find many features within the ruins which help us to date the buildings.

The first Norman castles were 'ringwork' single earthwork ramparts with timber palisades and an often prefabricated easy-to-assemble timber tower in the centre. Where possible, they took advantage of existing defences in old Roman forts (eg. Brough Castle in Cumbria).

After the Domesday Book of 1086, a glut of motte-and-bailey castles were built in strategic locations: in 1071 there had been thirty-three Norman castles built in England but by William's death in 1087 the number had more than doubled to eighty-six. Mottes were the rocky or man-made flat-topped mound where the defensive keep (the tower) was built. The level bailey area below contained timber buildings and the vital well and was surrounded by a palisaded earthwork bank and ditch. Pleshey in Essex is now bare of both tower and buildings but this makes it easy to see the scale of the motte-and-bailey earthworks. Square stone keeps soon replaced the timber towers. Often at least three storeys high, entry would always be by stairs directly into the main hall on the first floor, above which the top floors provided security for the private chambers for the lord.

In Scotland, stone castles began to be built in the 1100s. Rothesay on the Isle of Butte started as a twelfth-century keep set high on a motte and Castle Sween in Argyll is a solid example of a stone keep around a quadrangle – its gateway is set into walls that are 10ft thick.

A shell keep was a very tall, circular wall around the edge of the top of the motte. The most important castle buildings were nestled inside this wall. See a classic example at Totnes Castle in Devon).

Instead of square towers, more secure rounded towers developed from the late 1100s but inside they were cramped and awkward.

Curtain walls encircling the whole fort were designed to resist the huge stone-throwing catapults of the time. Being tactical as well as a simple blockade, several towers were built along the curtain wall. These were joined by walkways which had gaps linked by bridges which could be easily taken out of action to isolate individual towers from attack. Projecting rectangular towers with defensive arrow-slits were added to the curtain walls.

By the late 1200s, the classic medieval 'concentric' castle was in fashion. Edward I's campaigns in Wales built some of the best: polygonal outer stone walls now had huge fortified gatehouses with iron portcullises. Drawbridges crossed large surrounding moats, designed to prevent undermining of the walls by besieging armies. Barbicans were added to protect the gateways.

Machicolations ('murder holes') were openings in the gate roofs so that missiles could be lobbed through onto the attackers. Later, special platforms projected from the gate walls to form 'machicolated parapets'.

The wall walks were often crenellated and from the thirteenth century the openings of the crenellations were frequently protected by wooden shutters. By the late 1300s, castles had to contend with devastating attacks from small cannons and the system began to fail.

The late 1300s saw a flood of requests for licences to fortify private houses. During the late 1300s and the 1400s, tower houses were a regional version of fortified houses built in the Borders and Scotland and throughout Ireland. Rather like an isolated Norman keep, they often had just one room for each floor (although L-shaped and Z-shaped plans did develop in the post medieval era). They include the confusingly named pele towers or bastle houses which were just strong houses with pitched roofs (not tower-like at all in appearance). Being two to three storeys high, animals were housed in the lower floor and an external staircase led to the living areas.

In the 1400s, gatehouses were added to the keeps. They're easy to identify since they were often built in brick, not stone. By the 1500s, the firepower of artillery was making the medieval castle redundant.

Monasteries. A monastic revival changed the landscape from the eleventh century as Benedictines, Cistercians and Augustinians, amongst other orders, founded new houses throughout the land. Their dissolution in the 1530s would create the familiar and often very beautiful ruins that can be seen scattered across our countryside – their broken and scavenged ruins record their layout (the essence of which belonged firmly to their medieval origins) at the moment of their destruction. Frequently built to a set plan, the parts of even a very ruined monastery can often be easily identified.

The cross-shaped church, with its altar and grand window at the east end had transepts projecting to the north and south sides. The monks celebrated services east of this central crossing point, in the choir (quire) while the congregation remained (often standing) in the nave in the west end.

On the sheltered sunnier south side of the church lay the cloisters, a covered walkway around a grassy square. It was here that the monks lived their daily lives, reading aloud, scribing and even drying their laundry – not perhaps the haven of quiet we imagine. Around the cloisters were certain crucial rooms:

☞ **The sacristy** next to the church itself was where the valuable church 'plate' and vestments were kept. The Chapter House came next, where announcements were made and the monastic rules were read out daily.

☞ **Nearby** a small narrow room with benches was the parlour, often the only place where speaking was allowed in the silent orders.

☞ **A narrow passageway**, or slype, led out of the cloister.

☞ **The Warming House** can be identified by its often huge fireplace – you can stand up and walk around in the fireplace at Fountains Abbey in Yorkshire. This was the only fire in the monastery apart from in the kitchens.

☞ **Above the Warming House** (and benefiting from its heat) was the dormitory for the monks. It would run along the first floor on the east side of the cloister so that the monks could stumble down a night stair directly into the church for their night-time services.

☞ **At the end of the dormitory** was the essential latrine, or reredorter (meaning 'behind the dormitory'). These can be found placed over a stream, which acted as the main sewer.

☞ **The refectory** was the dining room. The monks ate in silence, which prompted a complex (and probably equally distracting) systems of signals to be invented to smooth the way for communal eating and the passing of bread. Improving texts would be read to the monks as they ate and in some monasteries you can still see the raised platform the reader would have stood on.

☞ **Often behind the refectory**, and always set apart to prevent the spread of fires, would be the kitchen.

☞ **The third, western side of the cloister** housed the lay brothers, who did all the work and farming rather than living a life of prayer and services. The usually large and grand Abbot's House can be found separate from the cloisters.

☞ **Again, set apart from the cloister** and usually on the eastern side of the church (often intriguingly and rather worryingly downstream from the monk's latrines) the infirmary was a long aisled building.

☞ **A gatehouse** ensured that the entrance to the monastery was duly grand, as befitted a wealthy landowner.

Strategically placed around their increasingly extensive lands, the monasteries owned granges (sometimes recalled in property names). These were the administrative centres for the monastery's profit-making ventures: sheep, mining, iron-working, wood and timber, crops and fish provided just some of their supplies and income. Indeed, fishponds can still be found marked on OS maps or spotted in the landscape.

Churches. Timber Saxon churches were ripped down and replaced by stone Norman churches. Built to impress the locals and to pass the test of time, a new distinctive church architecture was born. Its very specific styles progressed during the medieval ages, from plain Norman to the highly ornate Perpendicular style.

The first Norman churches had solid, massive masonry and semicircular or square eastern apses and round or square central towers. Romanesque rounded arches and semicircular arched windows and doorways were decorated with zigzag chevrons. Inside, the churches were plastered and the ceilings were barrel-vaulted.

From c.1170, increased wealth led to a showy Transitional Gothic or Pointed style in which windows and arches rose to a point and the ceilings were now rib-vaulted. The new proportions enabled higher and wider churches, prompting lantern towers containing windows to be built at the crossing to allow light into the dark centre of the church. Bell towers began to appear at the west end of churches and a north aisle, complete with a porch, might be added (the south side being occupied by graves).

From c.1220, the Early English Gothic phase produced stylised foliage decoration and ribbed vaulting in sections strengthened with stone arches, while spires began to be built onto towers. The windows became tall and narrow (lancet windows), pointed and usually without any tracery, and additional Lepers' windows peered into the south side of the choir while squints (also called hagioscopes) were set into the church to

St Margaret's church, Hales in Norfolk is an astonishingly pure Norman church.
(© Andrew Hovell)

TOP TIP

IDENTIFYING ROOF VAULTS

1066–1170:	Barrel vaults: looking like the inside of a half-barrel, they were like semi-circular long stone arches. Unable to span wide areas, they often needed buttresses to stabilise them. Sometimes two vaults crossed each other and these intersecting vaults were called groined vaults.
1170–1220:	Ribbed vaulting – as in Boxgrove Priory church in Sussex.
1220–1290:	Ribbed vaulting in sections, strengthened by stone arches.
1290–late 1300s:	More complex ceiling vaults (tierceron vaults).
1300s:	More ribs were added to create stellar patterns (lierne vaults).
1400s:	Yet more ribs were added to create fan-vaulted timber roofs with carved stone bosses at the rib intersections.

get round an obstructed view of the altar. Flying buttresses enabled thinner walls to be built (see Rievaulx Abbey's east end in Yorkshire).

From c.1290 the Decorated Gothic style brought in more and larger windows with more ornate thin tracery including stained glass rose window tracery in their apex. Ceiling vaultings became more complex. A couple of seats in the south wall of the chancel near the altar, together with a piscina for the priest's ritual washing, were sometimes added. South aisles were added to accommodate a growing population and pillars replaced the original wall.

From the late 1300s, right through to the 1500s, the Perpendicular Gothic style won the day. The pointed arches now became flatter 'four-centred' arches. Windows were often edged by a rectangular frame (as in Whitby's west end). Soaring fan-vaulted timber roofs were richly decorated (e.g. Melrose Abbey, Scotland) often matching the lavishness of the brightly painted interiors, statues, richly carved rood screen (supporting the 'rood' or cross) and reredos behind the altar and even the ornate candles. By the late 1400s very tall towers were added as grand personal gestures.

Bell-founding boomed from the 1400s and, due to their weight when finished, they were often made in bell-founding pits right beside the church.

Where to go

After the faint postholes of the Dark Age structures, we are suddenly deluged with medieval buildings and features to explore. Stone churches, castles, and monasteries abound.

Map of Britain: medieval sites.
(© Andrew Hovell)

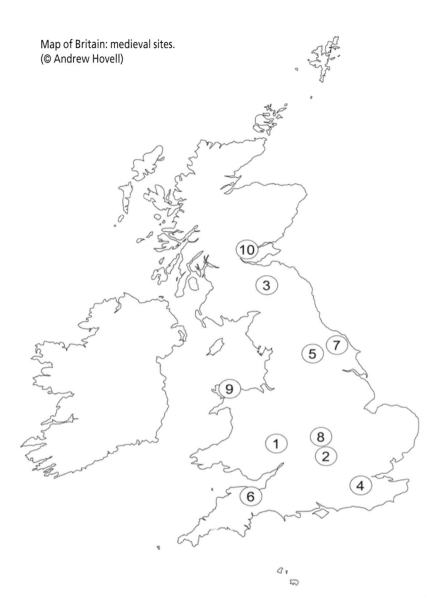

Kilpeck church

Romanesque churches have a restrained beauty all their own. Hereford and Worcester's Kilpeck church was built around 1140 and its nave, chancel and semicircular apse are typical of their time. Fantastic carvings survive around the arched south door and the west window. If you need evidence that Normans had a sense of humour and you want a laugh, look up and chuckle at the eighty-five stone carved animals and humans on the corbels around the top of walls – they were carved in the early twelfth century but their subjects are very Celtic indeed.

Iffley church

2 The Transitional Gothic style began in around 1170, at about the time that Iffley church near Oxford was built. Its narrow aisle-less structure and its south and west doors revelled in the earlier Romanesque finely carved decorations of mythical and Biblical creatures, foliage and men which accompanied the chevron carvings. But then the chancel was added in the Early English Gothic style in the 1200s – compare its simple pointed arches and slender stone pillars edging the windows.

The seats in the chancel of Iffley church were added at the end of the 1200s in the later Decorated Gothic style: notice how the fashionable *sedilia* priests' seats are more elaborate than the earlier windows. While you're here, take a look at the large perpendicular windows which were inserted in the fifteenth century and see how the old-style Romanesque arches were filled in.

Melrose Abbey

3 A grand example of the Perpendicular style is the ruined Melrose Abbey in Scotland. Rebuilt after 1385, ornate stone vaulting rises over the presbytery and its straight vertical lines, the window shapes and their delicate tracery are typical Perpendicular features. There are flying buttresses and plenty of stone details, such as the saints in the ceiling bosses and a famous gargoyle shaped like a pig playing the bagpipes.

A collage of church features display the styles of the a) Romanesque. Penmon Priory. (© Gillian Hovell) b) Early English Gothic decoration. St Mary the Virgin, Iffley. (© Les Hemsworth, with permission from the incumbent and churchwardens). c) Decorated Gothic sedilia. St Mary the Virgin, Iffley. (© Les Hemsworth, with permission of the incumbent and churchwardens) d) Perpendicular vaulting. (Melrose Abbey © Janis Heward)

Chaldon church

4 Chaldon church in Surrey contains the earliest known English wall painting and gives a taste of the power of the Norman church's teaching. The fresco in dark red and yellow ochre, dates from c.1200 and measures 17ft 3in x 11ft 2in. It depicts the 'Ladder of Salvation' which the good ascend to heaven but from which a demon tears wicked souls down to the gruesome, warning images of perpetrators of the seven deadly sins being tormented in Purgatory and Hell (*colour plate 26*). The message is clear: behave or be damned!

Yorkshire abbeys

5 To get a complete picture of the medieval ages, you simply have to visit at least one of the great abbeys of the time. The pick of the best are Rievaulx and Fountains Cistercian abbeys in Yorkshire, Tintern's superbly situated Gothic Cistercian house in Wales, and Jedburgh's Augustinian Romanesque and Gothic priory on the Borders. Fountains Abbey in North Yorkshire has it all though – follow the guide to features in the 'What to Look For' section and take a tour through the monks' lives.

Dunster Village

6 To see an abbey tithe barn, Dunster village in Exmoor National Park has a repaired one as a community building which you can look at from the outside – but put your walking shoes on and tour the village's mass of medieval buildings while you're there. There's a pack horse bridge, a heavily walled circular dovecote once belonging to a priory founded in the twelfth century, a working watermill, a castle (originating in the eleventh century) with its fifteenth-century gatehouse (National Trust), the fifteenth-century nunnery, and the largely fifteenth-century church still with its 54ft-long rood screen and built around its eleventh-century west door and north wall.

Wharram Percy

7 Wharram Percy is a stunning example of a deserted medieval village. Go on a clear day when the sun is low in winter and you'll be able to see the ghostly outlines of building plots much easier. Don't linger too long as the sun goes down though – it's a 0.75-mile walk back to the car!

Wharram Percy captured in a low sunlight. (© Andrew Hovell)

Shuckburgh

8　Medieval ridge and furrow can be seen in many places but there are some fine examples in Shuckburgh (Warwickshire) and Ludgershall near Aylesbury.

Beaumaris Castle

9　We have so many wonderful castles across Britain that we are spoilt for choice, but if you want to see a castle that's a snapshot of a particular time, you can't do better than Beaumaris on Anglesey – as one of Edward I's Welsh campaign castles, it was built 'all new' but it was never quite finished, never used, and therefore never suffered the slings and arrows of refurbishment. It has everything that a traditional child's castle would have: an impressive gatehouse, a drawbridge, a wall with towers you can climb up, surrounded by a moat, high walkways and winding staircases. Add a pale-stoned chapel, grassy courtyards and corridors snaking through the thick walls and you have a classic day out set in the thirteenth century.

Alloa Tower

10　The tower houses were a regional version of fortified houses built in the Borders and Scotland and throughout Ireland during the late fourteenth and fifteenth centuries. Alloa Tower in central Scotland was completed in 1497 and is one of the largest of its type. You can see the original oak roof beams and internal wall, and the medieval groin vaulting.

Beaumaris curtain wall. (© Gillian Hovell)

What life was like

The arrival of the Normans put a whole new set of people into all the places and positions of power: the new King, his nobles and his administrators (civil service in effect) all belonged to a new age – even the priests were ousted by Norman replacements. These new overlords spoke Norman French and wrote their prodigious laws, records and diplomatic communications in Latin, thus making Britain tri-lingual as the plebs continued to speak Old English: not for them the filth of 'cows' herded by locals in the field, but ready-prepared Old French's *boef* (our 'beef') on the table and an account of *boves* (our 'bovine') recorded in the Latin of the Domesday Book.

That Domesday Book gives us a precious glimpse of life in 1086: an observer of the time wrote that 'there was no single hide nor a yard of land, nor indeed one ox nor one cow nor one pig which was left out.' It must have been like encountering the taxman, computerised records, CCTV and the sword all combined in one.

Despite the culture shock, there was little doubt over who was in control. Within four years of the Conquest, the Normans had brutally smashed resistance in Northumbria and by 1086 they had entered Wales. This rapid expansion was made possible by forcibly drafting the locals into the building of the new castles. With equal speed, the old Saxon churches were torn down, graveyards trashed and stone Romanesque churches put up in their place. It was from these powerbases that the local Norman lords dispensed their own law and order.

This new nobility was in the minority (about a dozen lords held a quarter of England) and these favoured few led a life full of fighting and feasting (*colour plate 27*). Hunting, once the sport of everyman was now for the privileged alone: deer parks were created, forcing locals who lived in an area that could be hundreds of acres, from their homes.

Those homes had been scattered homesteads and villages for centuries. But now they came under new Norman management and the rigid feudal system in England now had new lords. While the King owned the land, he granted bits of it to those barons and church leaders who had come with him from France and had supported him and they in turn loaned it to those below them and so on, with the peasants virtually at the bottom of the heap: they could live in their homes only as long as they paid rent (either in cash or in kind) and worked the land for the lord of the manor and gave him a high proportions of the produce. The only people lower than the peasants were slaves.

Every aspect of life seemed to involve deferment to superiors. Even grinding your own corn was banned – you had to take it to the licensed mill and pay them to grind it. No peasant married without his lord's consent. It wasn't until the thirteenth century that law even began to work for the benefit of the common man instead of being a means of asserting power.

Law had been based on Trial by Ordeal but now the sword-wielding Normans added Trial by Battle too – the pre-eminence of those with the best war skills reminds us that the Normans had once been Norsemen and came from the same Germanic warrior stock as the Scandinavian Vikings and Anglo-Saxons. Thankfully, sworn juries entered the legal world in the twelfth century but it was still unrecognisably wobbly as a fair form of justice. A century on, the law of precedent and the use of receipts were helping to level the playing field – the Norman obsession with paperwork was the dawning of modern bureaucracy.

The efficient Norman administration did spark a resurgence of urban living. In the thirteenth century, old towns were growing and new ones were being developed: inns, shops, houses, market places, market crosses, wells, wharves and cathedrals multiplied – all under the gaze of stone castles.

In Wales, too, the economy was developing and the population probably doubled between 1050 and 1300. Forests were cleared, villages expanded. They took to building forts like the Normans and by 1200 every major Welsh area had a Cistercian monastery (like those at Strata Florida and Vale Crucis).

For, across the land, a monastic revival was underway. A landscape that a century earlier had held nothing except small timber buildings was now pockmarked with towering castles and a selection of monasteries. As the King and his nobles gave land to the Church, as a part-payment for a place in heaven, others followed the fashion. Soon the Church was recruiting small armies of lay brothers to till their land, tend their valuable flocks and man a variety of industrial enterprises, all with a highly developed sense of big business. Natural resources were closely guarded and carefully maintained: coppicing and pollarding of trees ensured a flow of timber and wood and mining rights were monitored – all that was on or under the land was theirs.

Edwards I's campaigns into Scotland and Wales were raising higher tax burdens and the Scots responded with raids into northern England - and the border lands became a place of terror and tower houses. Meanwhile, the Hundred Years War was warming up, taking men and adding still further to the taxes. Nonetheless, trade had been flourishing – England had been the main supplier of high-quality wool to Europe and the Lord Chancellor symbolically sat on a woolsack – but the travel it promoted was about to bring death and horror to Britain. Not only did the climate worsen and crops repeatedly fail causing famine, but plague arrived on a ship – within two years it had devastated the population. '1350. The people who remain are driven wild and miserable' cries the sombre graffiti in St Mary's in Ashwell, Hertfordshire.

Suddenly manpower was no longer plentiful – tenants may not have been poached by neighbouring lords but, as society fell apart, they certainly voted with their feet and headed for better conditions elsewhere. Many opted for the chance of earning a living in a trade in the developing towns and whole villages were deserted, destroyed by both plague and economic pressure.

As the common people tasted a newfound freedom from their lords they began to acquire a voice. And that voice shouted when the poll tax was levied in the late 1300s: it sparked rebellion for how could the poorest pay the same as the rich? There were certainly plenty of poor. Life in the towns had proved to be no get-rich-quick fix. Begging and prostitution were rife – indeed the slum town cottages called *bordelli* gave rise to our 'bordellos'.

The Church who had cared for the poor found that its inability to defeat the plague had cost it its authority on several fronts: the new guilds provided spiritual as well as practical relief; Wycliffe's English Bible put the Word of God into the hands of the common people to interpret as they saw fit; and while the fat cat abbeys struggled to regain their position, the reclusive orders rose in popularity – their isolation had spared them but their survival seemed more like a judgement from on high. Carthusian priories like Mount Grace in Yorkshire were established in this aftershock and the ruined hermit cells can still be visited today.

In this post-plague world the rules were changing: social climbing was on the up. Those guilds supported enterprise and individuals could now rise in status. Better, half-timbered houses or even brick ones were being built and glass windows were a regular feature. Meanwhile, tension had been festering in Wales. At the end of the century Owain Glyn Dwr waged war, demanding Welsh freedom from English dominion.

By 1500, the English longbow had reigned triumphant, only to be supplemented by crossbows and finally replaced by gunpowder and cannons which could rip through existing defences. The Norman castles, which had stood guard for 400 years, were obsolete. But this was only one of the many changes over the last 400 years. Britain had begun the medieval ages locked in a feudal society but that system could not survive the nightmares of the fourteenth century. Like the phoenix rising from the ashes, a new social and political order was staggering to its feet.

Things to do

It's worth going to Hastings to see where it all began. It may be just a battlefield, but it's archaeology in the raw – the events that happened here in 1066 changed Britain's history for ever. There is a new interactive visitor experience that brings it to life: try a shield and chain-mail for size, watch a dramatic film and take an audio tour as you walk the battlefield and stand where King Harold fell and Anglo-Saxon England died.

Likewise, the Royal Armouries in Leeds isn't just for military historians. Go and see the armoury of the medieval days – check the events diary and watch a choreographed display of knights' swordsmanship as they explain the niceties of staying alive. And it's all free.

Many medieval buildings were made of timber and therefore few have survived. However, at Weald and Downland Open Air Museum in West Sussex there is a fascinating collection of nearly fifty medieval and later buildings which have been rescued from destruction and re-erected here. Pop into the thirteenth-century rural lord's cottage with its single-hearthed living area and a kitchen with a stone oven. Note the single small window and how, like Iron Age roundhouses, the smoke filtered out through the thatch. Poorer folk shared wattle-and-daub huts with their animals for security and warmth. Go to www.wealdown.co.uk

Weald and Downland Open Air Museum is a chance to walk into another age. (Reproduced with permission of Weald and Downland Open Air Museum)

Barley Hall in York is a medieval townhouse that has been lovingly restored to expose its original glorious high ceilings, timber frames and a unique horn. Decorated in the style for the Sawsell home in 1483, visitors can step over the high doorsills and wander through the building, making themselves at home and handling objects and sitting on the chairs and benches. Check out the visitor details and download a walk-through guide on www.barleyhall.org.uk

Be a medieval monk for a day! Don the white robes of the Cistercians of Fountains Abbey and head out with a guide into the ruins where the real monks lived and prayed.

Museums with especially strong medieval displays are Lancaster City Museum, the East Midlands' Derby Museum and Art Gallery, Leicester's Jewry Wall Museum and Norwich's Castle Museum.

Charcoal fuelled medieval Britain. So much so that south England was virtually stripped of trees to fuel the iron industry needed for the Tudor wars. In the Forest of Dean you can watch traditional charcoal burners demonstrating their work. Phone the Dean Heritage Centre on 01594 822170 to check what dates they're operating. The Centre also displays the Forest of Dean's medieval hunting forest heritage, as well as its later mining and industrial history. The library on site holds thousands of archives, making it a perfect place to get familiar with archive digging.

At the end of the medieval period the warship the *Mary Rose* was doing fine service. A symbol and tool of Henry's thirst for war with France, she was the ultimate war machine – she survived sea battles only to sink in 1545 due to undisciplined mariners who left the gun ports open and so allowed water to pour into her belly – 500 men drowned that day. The raising of the *Mary Rose,* nearly 440 years later in 1982, was televised and the world held its breath as she lurched in the salvage rigging. Her preservation has given us a unique piece of archaeology, full of so many eye-opening personal finds that went down with her: lanterns, manicure sets, rosary beads and embossed book covers – a snapshot in time of a country at war and the mariners who lived and died in her. You can find out more on www.maryrose.org

If one battle heralded the start of the medieval age, another closed it: the Battle of Bosworth put Henry VII on the throne as the first Tudor king and change was afoot. The Bosworth Battlefield Heritage Centre and Country Park in Nuneaton re-lives this important event and shares the archaeological skills needed to find the battlefield and interpret what documentary evidence, osteo-archaeology, sampling and analysis can tell us. Wander through the reconstruction buildings too to catch the mood of the time.

Reading up

For a quick starter guide to medieval life, look at John Gillingham and Ralph Griffiths' *Medieval Britain: A Very Short Introduction* (Oxford Paperbacks). For a really easy introduction to medieval life, you could do far worse than flick through the Dorling Kindersley *Eyewitness Guide: Medieval Life*. Don't be put off by the fact that it's a children's guide – it's an excellent way to discover the pertinent facts about the age.

Television historian, Michael Wood celebrated the 900th anniversary of the Domesday Book with his story of how the English world changed when the Normans arrived in *Domesday: A Search for the Roots of England* (BBC Publications 1986).

Justin Pollard's *Seven Ages of Britain* (Hodder & Stoughton 2003) contains a fascinating look at daily life in the medieval world, while Robert Lacey's and Danny Danziger's *The Year 1000: What Life was like at the Turn of the First Millennium* (Little, Brown & company 1999) gives a longer, closer and very evocative look at medieval life.

Archaeology-rooted studies are John Steane's *The Archaeology of Medieval England and Wales* (Croom Helm 1984) and David Hinton's worthy *Archaeology, Economy and Society* (Routledge 1990).

Specialist topics abound, such as James Grimswold's *Tithe Barns of England: A Guide for the Traveler* (University Press of New England 1999). Detailed writings can be found in Anthony Quinney's *The Traditional Buildings of England* (Thames and Hudson 1990), Colin Platt's *The English Medieval Town* (Secker & Warburg 1976), Patrick Ottaway's *The Archaeology of British Towns* (Routledge 1992), N.J.G. Pounds' *The Medieval Castle* (Leicester University Press 1990) and Nigel Ramsey's *English Medieval Industries* (Hambledon Press 1991).

The Batsford/Historic Scotland series includes a general book on *Medieval Scotland* (Peter Yeoman, 1995) as well as books on *Scottish Castles* (Chris Tabraham 1997) and *Scottish Cathedrals* (Richard Fawcett 1997). Explore medieval iron-working by logging onto websites such as my own community archaeology project, Iron-Age (Nidderdale)'s www.iron-age.org

For a light taste of medieval life, try some novels set in the Middle Ages: Ellis Peters' *Cadfael* series centre around a fictional worldly-wise lay-brother's life at a monastery and her *The Brothers of Gwynedd* (under her real name of Edith Pargetter) brings Medieval Wales to life.

POST MEDIEVAL, INDUSTRIAL AND MODERN AGE

INTRODUCTION

In the early 1500s, Britain was striding blindfold towards a cliff edge. Since Henry VII had won the crown at the Battle of Bosworth in 1485 he had spent his reign avoiding war, encouraging trade and striving for better order in Wales and the north. He had improved administration and increased royal wealth (even if his methods had dramatically failed to garner public goodwill). By 1509, Britain was relatively united and certainly solvent. But a hidden abyss lay ahead.

Henry VIII was the antithesis of his father. War was virtually a passionate hobby for him, and his understanding of national economy reached as far as his own feast-laden table. He duly fought the Scots (defeating them in the Battle of Flodden in 1513), campaigned against France and, when the Pope refused to grant his divorce and then excommunicated him for going ahead with his marriage to Anne Boleyn anyway, he broke with Rome.

The medieval ways of life were about to be ripped from the heart of England. The Reformation would cast down the rich monasteries. These powerhouses had controlled the local rhythm of life for generations, for centuries even, but now, virtually overnight the abbots and monks were pensioned off and the grand abbeys stripped down to their stone skeletons. While the King's commissioners surveyed the land and evaluated its riches, a general free-for-all occurred: yeoman farmers and families acquired the lands in the knowledge that they could become the new dominant locals. Scotland's Reformation came a little later through John Knox's preaching, but it was just as swift and sure.

The following decades would require some nimble religious foot-shuffling by ministers and the common people alike as the country swung from Protestant to Catholic and back again. Being on the wrong side of the Prayer Book or the Mass led to a fiery damnation in the here-and-now as the smoke and stench from the burning of heretics at the stakes regularly filled the air.

Henry's wars turned into Elizabeth I's wars: Spain and Ireland's civil wars kept the English fleets and troops busy. Artillery had made the Norman castles obsolete and Henry VIII had urgently built new cannon-proof forts. Now whole regions of woodlands were destroyed as timber warships were launched into the bloodied seas and as charcoal was devoured to fuel the smelting and forging of ever more iron weapons. New industrial scale of blast furnaces abounded as industry became a well-trodden route to private fortunes.

When Elizabeth died in 1603, James VI of Scotland became James I, King of England and Ireland in the 'Union of the Crowns'. This joint role required fine juggling skills – the Calvinist Scots, Catholic Irish and Protestant English all had very different hopes and dreams (and nightmares) – but James lacked tact: he even lectured his own countrymen on the 'superiority of English civilisation'. The insecure Catholics in England resorted to the Gunpowder Plot, which would have put an end to King and Parliament alike had it succeeded. Having survived though, James' lasting legacy was to be the King James's Authorised Version of the Bible – it would remain the language of the Church for over 250 years.

Charles I took the throne and managed to upset just about everyone: he fought the Scots when they rose up over his enforcement of a new prayer book, the Catholic Irish when they rebelled and, eventually the English Parliament itself when he tried to arrest certain MPs in 1642. The Civil War raged on, dividing families and the nations, even after Cromwell and a rump of MPs had Charles arrested and executed in 1649. Cromwell's radical professional New Model Army went on to crush Scottish and Irish resistance but he died in 1658 having held the office of Lord Protector of the new Commonwealth of England, Scotland and Ireland for just five years. In 1660, Charles II was duly invited out of exile. At this point emotion spilled over and Cromwell's body was dug up from Westminster Cathedral, hung in chains and beheaded: this was a man who had made enemies.

But Charles II's rule would be far from easy. Within a few years, London would be torn apart by the plague and the Great Fire; his moody relationship with Parliament ended in his dissolution of it in 1681, and his obsessions with his mistresses constantly marred his public image. Yet, when he died in 1685, trade and colonisation had expanded in India, the East Indies and America, and Britain was ready to rule the waves.

As the seventeenth century drew to a close, James II stepped in and shook the already rickety religious and political foundations by seeming to favour Catholicism. Terror spread. His daughter, Mary, had married William of Orange and the English Protestants enlisted his eager aid – James II fled when the army sided with the newcomer, and William and Mary took the throne in 1677. However, neither they nor James' II's Protestant daughter, Anne, had any heirs. The Act of Settlement in 1701 hastily dictated that the Protestant Hanoverian line from James I's granddaughter would succeed after Anne – thus excluding James I's Catholic descendants. Furthermore, in 1707 England and Scotland were formally united in the 'Union of Parliaments' so that when Anne died in 1714, Hanoverian George I succeeded as King of the United Kingdom of Great Britain.

Not everyone was happy. The Scottish Jacobites wanted a Stuart back on the throne and the battles raged, until the final blow was struck by the English at Culloden in 1746. By then, thirty years of fighting had stained numerous battlefields and the war zone had seen the construction of many Hanoverian military roads, forts and bridges.

Meanwhile, British colonies were spreading, but the American War of Independence resulted in thirteen colonies being lost to Britain in 1783. Nonetheless, worldwide trade, naval power and public borrowing via the Bank of England created a very commercially-minded Britain in which enterprise was encouraged. During the five Hanoverian monarchs (four Georges and William), Britain would enter the industrial age and her society would change beyond all recognition.

In the early 1800s new defensive landmarks were peppering the south coast as the Napoleonic wars created a very real threat of invasion by the self-crowned Emperor of France. In 1801, despite the uncertainty of the future, the Act of Union dissolved the Irish Parliament and created the new United Kingdom of Great Britain and Ireland.

The industrial revolution continued to steam ahead. Thousands flocked to work in the new factories and the towns expanded at an unprecedented speed. When Victoria became queen in 1837, the eighteen year old was faced with a troubled Britain: disease ran amok in the overcrowded towns; her rural Irish subjects barely survived the first Potato Famine in 1846; further blights continued and reached Scotland where the Scottish Clearances had been causing terrible grief since the end of the previous century. However, by the end of her reign in 1901, Britain would have a thriving Empire and would lead the world in industry and commerce.

The World Wars, interspersed with the Depression, changed the world yet again as scientific advancements were eagerly sought to provide military supremacy. The fabric of society was ripped apart and rebuilt not once but twice.

MOVING ON

By 1945, the old ways had been blasted away and a new world was being rebuilt on the ruins of lives that had gone before. Those ruins stretched right back into Victorian industrial urbanisation. Then back further to the struggles of an emerging united Britain and beyond, to the formation of our medieval villages, the Germanic invaders and Latin-speaking Romans with their forts and infrastructures. Even back to the roundhouses and early monument builders who first settled down into communities or to those distant ancestors who followed the migrating herds into our lands.

Whatever land we build now, we build it on the foundations of those societies that went before us. We can look around us and see the archaeology – the physical reminders – of those countless lives that went before us, the progress and changes that occurred as time rolled on and which created the landscape we live in today. And when we can look around us and recognise those features from the past that we live alongside every day, we can sense our place in the continuing story that is Britain.

Obviously, the archaeology dating from the years between 1500 and the twentieth century varies considerably, stretching as it does from the last vestiges of the medieval days, through the Tudor renaissance and into the heavyweight industrial remains and the scars from the World Wars. However, each of these phases has its own special features that can be used to identify their date.

Ruined monasteries and abbeys are wonderfully scenic and romantic places to visit and it is easy to forget the cultural vandalism that took place in the 1530s. These ruins are a record, literally set in stone, of the buildings that stood at the moment of dissolution. Check out the monastic features in the Medieval Era section.

Churches bear scars from the Reformation days. Ripped-out features such as altar rails, icons and whitewashed wall paintings often left a faint trace on the wall or an empty niche behind.

Look for 'Laird's Lofts'; galleries that were fitted into churches for the gentry in the 1600s/1700s in Scotland. Two good examples are at St Bridget's Kirk in Dalgety in Fife, and St Peter's church in Duffus in Grampian.

The Disruption in the Scottish Presbyterian Church forced meetings to be held outside the locked churches. Look out for the little amphitheatres of stone seats, like the terracing at Am Ploc by Torridon (c.1843) that were built as a result.

On the military front, Henry VIII hurriedly built artillery forts to fend off the enemy's new cannons. The harbours of the south coast of England has numerous examples of these multi-sided thick-curtain walled, squat structures. State-of-the-art design included an angled wall line, which enabled every part of the fort to be protected by gunfire.

In Scotland, the tower houses were extended into L-shapes and Z-shapes. Ground-floor kitchens and cellars with tiny secure windows sat below the first floor main hall and above that were the private rooms and a walkway around the roof. Elcho Castle in Tayside was built to this standard layout in 1590 and the later 1620s Craigievar Castle still has many original fixtures to admire: a walled courtyard, the iron gate at the entrance, and even the 1620s plaster ceilings.

Major-General Wade's military roads, complete with stone bridges fording the rivers (e.g. Wade's Bridge at Aberfeldy), carried the Hanoverian armies into Scotland during the Jacobite rebellions (although, ironically, the first army to use the Wade Road over the Corryairick Pass was that of the Jacobites).

Seating terraces at Am Ploc provided outdoor worship areas during the Disruption. (© Liz Forrest)

At the start of the nineteenth century, over 100 Martello towers watched for the impending Napoleonic invasion. Copied from a design which had enabled two small cannons to humiliate a British army's 106-gun power siege in Corsica, they were small, thick-walled towers, topped with a big gun.

Tudor houses bear a number of giveaway features:

- 👁 **Half-timbered houses** were built on a wooden frame (the black timbers) which was filled with patterned brick (herringbone was popular) or, if you couldn't afford that, white stucco plaster. Beware the modern 'mock Tudor' lookalikes.
- 👁 **Chimneys** (often heavy in appearance, being several twisting corkscrew styled stacks clustered together) appear for the first time.
- 👁 **Roofs** were steeply pitched.
- 👁 **Doorways** and the typical tall narrow windows preferred a flattened arch to the earlier pointed Gothic style and were often capped by simple squared-off mouldings.
- 👁 **Oriel windows** are strikingly Tudor – these large, multi-sided windows projected out from an upper floor and were supported by a corbel (bracket) – but notice that the glass panes themselves remain small (*colour plate 28*).
- 👁 **Upper floors** could overhang the front of the house, especially in towns were space was at a premium.
- 👁 **Inside**, oak wood panelling was a favoured decor and could reach floor-to-ceiling.
- 👁 **New brick** gatehouses with a broad low arch flanked by towers were often built for show.

Half-timbered late fifteenth-century hall-house in Downland Open Air Museum near Chichester. (Reproduced with permission of Weald and Downland Open Air Museum)

Increasingly, money was used to display wealth not to fortify it: dovecotes provided eggs and winter meat for the wealthy and were a true status symbol. The family who acquired Penmon Priory in Anglesey after its dissolution built a square domed stone dovecote – you can sense the social showing off involved in the stone cliff-style nests for over a thousand birds. Its scale meant it required ascending a 3.5m- (12ft-) high central stone pillar to reach many of them.

Elizabethan prosperity created a glut of new country houses being built and older Tudor manor houses were remodelled along new lines. Influenced by the Italian Renaissance, in came curved gables, formal gardens and a symmetrical layout on a long E-shaped design with a central entrance and upstairs 'long gallery'. Favoured classical designs squared off the windows and the grouped chimney stacks.

Stone, not brick, was again in fashion and the universal decoration inside and out was strap work, carved in low relief or moulded in plaster into symmetrical geometric patterns.

Occasional Renaissance showing-off bubbled up, as at Edzell Castle Gardens in Tayside where the walled garden laid out in 1604 incorporates carvings of the Liberal Arts, Cardinal Virtues and Planetary gods – all good fun. Proud yeoman farmers inscribed their initials and, conveniently for us, the date of the house over the main door.

Eighteenth-century estates boasted ice houses which were sunk below ground and included a watertight stone or brick pit (with drainage from its base) in which ice collected from the estate land was stored. Domed roofs were normal and the 'posher' versions had cavity walls. By the nineteenth century they were only partially buried or built above ground and were built conveniently near the house – their wooden shelves held commercially-packed ice (which could last a year if stored between straw).

A remnant from the past, this ice house stands by a public footpath in Gairloch, Scotland. (© Liz Forrest)

At the other end of the scale, the poor on the Scottish estates were being cleared out. When walking in deserted Scottish highland areas, keep an eye out for abandoned stone-built settlements which may be crofts or could be the relics of fashionable sporting estates for the new monied industrialists.

In remote areas of course, pre-industrial poor dwellings continued unaffected by change – the blackhouse on the isle of Lewis was built in the 1800s and lived in until 1945 (now an unmissable museum), while astonishing cave rock-houses at Kinver Edge were lived in from medieval times right up to the 1950s.

Sheilings are found in Scotland: these deserted stone huts were temporary summer accommodation for herdsman in upland or marginal land. Their ruins rarely survive as more than drystone or turf humps in the ground but occasionally they may have circular structures set into their north side as a cool store for dairy produce.

Mining tore apart the land but over the centuries the earth reclaims it and it can be surprisingly difficult to spot. Early adit mines drove horizontally into the hillside – look for a fan of spoil at the end of a trench leading straight into the hillside.

After c.1500, shaft mines were made by digging vertically into the ground – the spoil from the shaft was piled up around the shaft entrance so that it resembled a doughnut with a hole (*colour plate 29*). Avoid standing in the

An abandoned sheiling – hardly a spacious home, it was barely 8ft long (© Liz Forrest)

dimple in the centre of these now grassed-over mounds – a few rotting planks and a pile of earth and rubbish may be all that stands between you and a drop of a hundred feet! Nonetheless, look out for a series of these 'doughnuts' as the shafts were sunk along a seam of coal or other mineral.

From c.1600 blast furnaces belched out smoke and produced iron for the up-and-coming industrial and commercial age. Their ruins are heavy square, windowless towers with big arches, clearly industrial in purpose. Keep your eye on the ground for pieces of the black, bubbly waste material of iron making, the slag.

From the 1830s railways spread across the land but many were removed in Dr Beeching's cuts in the 1960s. OS maps still mark disused railway line and raised embankments can still be found – many a public footpath or cycle track (such as the Camel Trail in Cornwall) runs along their level, flat ridges, edged by rosebay willow herb plants. Look closely and you may spot an old railway sleeper still poking out of the grass. 'Old Station Inn' pubs may mark the long-closed stations.

Even as the railways were carving up the landscape, the Enclosure Acts were giving birth to England's 'patchwork quilt' of fields. The centuries' old pattern of little fields with wiggly walls and the open pastures was being replaced by squares.

The land was parcelled up – look out for strictly rectangular blocks of fields, bounded by fences or (in Yorkshire and Derbyshire especially) drystone walls of prescribed heights, widths and construction. They are often obvious when they edge into open moorland.

Especially wide ridges in a field can look like medieval ridge and furrow marks: however, if they are framed by an encircling furrow, or have very narrow (2–3m) ridges they are probably a product of later nineteenth-century steam ploughing. Good examples of the wide ridges can be seen from the A14 at Naseby in Northamptonshire and in Kent while the narrow ridges are most common around Manchester and in Cheshire.

The archaeology of the World Wars is rapidly disappearing and it would be neither possible nor desirable to preserve all the sites. Key sites which will best inform future generations are fighting to be maintained but here are some of the features which are quietly blending into our landscape:

- ◉ **Coastal defences** included pillboxes: look for their splayed horizontal gun slits for greatest covering fire. Bembridge on the Isle of Wight has one built into the newer sea defences (*colour plate 30*) and several are preserved, disguised among the fallen masonry of the Roman fort at Pevensey.
- ◉ **Concrete blocks** acted as tank traps (such as those around Blanford Forum in Dorset, Graveney Marsh in Kent or near the River Ock in Oxfordshire).
- ◉ **Second World War underground operations rooms**, tunnels and lookouts: Dover is the famous one.

- **Airfields** with technical sites and military housing nearby (e.g. Kenley aerodrome in Surrey where the runways are grassing over, but Biggin Hill in Surrey remains in use).
- **Anti-aircraft gun emplacements** (as at Cobham and many other coastal sites in Kent).
- **Early warning systems** such as the concrete dishes called Sound Mirrors (e.g. Abbot's Cliff and Hythe in Kent) were superseded by RADAR.
- **An infrastructure** of supply depots, research establishments and bunkers.
- **POW camps**: Harperley camp in Co. Durham was championed by Michael Wood in BBC2's *Restoration* programme.
- **Civil defence shelters**: Anderson shelters of corrugated iron still lurk at the bottom of a number of suburban gardens.

Where to go

Map of Britain: post-medieval and industrial sites. (© Andrew Hovell)

Churches

(1) If you're visiting Iffley church near Oxford for its Norman architecture, take a look at a staircase set into the right-hand wall during the fifteenth century – it led to a rood loft, which supported a beam across the church which in turn held a large crucifix (rood). Such roodscreens were removed during the Reformation.

(2) The simple Langley Chapel (Shropshire) dates largely to c.1546 but, like all other churches, its sixteenth-century fittings were stripped out. It still has an almost full set of early seventeenth-century Puritan timber fittings though – this plain style is what replaced the ceiling paintings, the icons and rood screens.

Houses

(3) The greatest Tudor house to use the new, luxury material of brick was Hampton Court Palace. This palace, fit even for a king as opulent as Henry VIII, is stuffed full of Tudor features. Follow the building's development as the Stuarts and then William and Mary make it their own with the latest fashions of their time – window and door shapes, chimneys, gardens, extensions … it's all here.

Military

(4) Henry VIII himself designed one of the artillery forts and Southsea Castle (Hampshire), completed in 1544, might be it. Restored almost to its original condition this is a fun fort with plenty of features to explore and an exhibition, visual displays and a 'tunnel walk' as well.

(5) The Jacobite rising of 1745 prompted a rush of state-of-the-art military fortifications. Fort George near Inverness is still in use by the military so access is limited, but nonetheless it's a great place to see its circuit of massive earthen ramparts, faced with stone walls, which were designed to absorb artillery impacts. Entry was across a bridge over an outer moat onto an island and then a longer bridge across a wider, inner moat. 'Casements' were bomb-proof, brick-vaulted barracks beneath the ramparts which could shelter an entire garrison.

(6) One of the two Hackness Martello towers on the island of Hoy has been restored and you can visit its eerie small-windowed barrack room on the first floor (unnervingly above the powder magazine, storeroom and water cistern) and peruse its on-site displays.

TOP TIP

Hurst Castle, Hampshire has a wealth of Tudor details, like arches and windows: finished in 1544, its twelve-sided keep and three big bastions were built to house seventy-one guns. Unfortunately the king could only afford twenty. (Note, however, that the vaults were added in 1803 to support larger guns, and the huge gun batteries on either side of the original keep were built in the 1850s).

Palmerston forts still stand watch over the Solent (© Palmerston Forts Society)

7 In the 1840-'60s a chain of artillery forts were built next to all major ports. Expensive to build, they were outdated before they were finished – these were the doomed Palmerston forts, built in red brick, mostly underground with great earth banks and tunnels. The best example is Fort Brockhurst in Portsmouth where the parade ground, gun ramps and moated keep can all be visited. It also happens to be the store for English Heritage's extensive reserve collection and you can take a sneaky behind-the-scenes tour of this valuable collection. Ferries now peacefully pass a couple of Palmerston forts in the Solent.

8 Dover's White Cliffs house the labyrinth of secret wartime tunnels, where Dunkirk was masterminded. Here you'll be bombarded by sights, sounds and Pathe news clips that bring the story dramatically to life and you can tour the underground wartime hospital. Arrive early to avoid disappointment – visitor numbers are limited.

Industry

9 Click mills were simple water mills whose horizontal paddle-wheel directly drove the millstone. Dounby on Orkney had a restored example: although introduced by the Norse settlers, this type of mill continued in use into the 1900s – a salutary reminder that not all industrial techniques become obsolete at the same speed in different areas.

The Click Mill at Dounby stands testimony to the unchanging nature of life in remote areas. (© Liz Forrest)

10 Ironbridge Gorge, on the other hand, is *the* birthplace of the industrial revolution (*colour plate 31*). Abraham Darby's furnace in Coalbrookdale where it all began is just a part of one of the ten award-winning museums along this beautiful valley. One day here is simply not enough to explore all this leafy gorge has to offer.

11 Bonawe ironworks in Argyll are the most complete example of charcoal-fuelled ironworks in Britain, having a very well-preserved furnace and vast charcoal sheds. Established in 1752-3 by Richard Ford, the company created a whole infrastructure for its workers: houses, a school and a church were built.

12 A surviving (and still inhabited) example of such a factory community is New Lanark's eighteenth-century cotton mill village in southern Scotland. This outstanding restored monument is a World Heritage Site. Discover how a visionary mill manager, Robert Owen, transformed industrial life here: decent homes instead of slums housed the workers who were provided with schools, evening classes, free health care and affordable food – and child labour and corporal punishment was banned. This was revolutionary stuff.

The Bedlam blast furnace at Ironbridge Gorge (© Andrew Hovell)

What was life like?

In 1500, Christopher Columbus had just landed in the Caribbean and a brave new world that had never been seen by before by Europeans was on the horizon. At home, most people's thoughts must rarely have strayed so far. England was still licking its wounds after forty years of civil war in the Wars of the Roses, and the Borders and Scotland were rife with battles. To the west, the Welsh were a force to be reckoned with but Henry VIII's Act of Union in 1536 enforced English law there and tried to insist that the English language was used in administrative affairs.

Language was a touchy subject at the time. Tyndale had printed his English New Testament in 1526, weakening the Church's steely grip on Bible interpretation as the common plebs began to study the Word of God for themselves.

The Church was already staggering: it hadn't recovered from its failure to stop the plague in its tracks in the mid 1300s and Henry VIII's split from Rome in 1534 started a religious see-saw in England which would divide the faithful in Britain for generations. Then came the Dissolution of the Monasteries: as Henry cut their purse strings and gorged on their commandeered fortunes, the Church's power was hamstrung. As the Reformation took hold, every altar was nervously stripped, the icons vanished almost overnight and wall paintings were rapidly painted over.

The medieval world was being whitewashed but hundreds of years of traditions didn't die quietly – when Edward VI dissolved chantries, where the comforting and very Catholic prayers to ameliorate purgatory were said, the west country rebelled in 1549 with a shocking violence of spirit and body as the king's commissioners were murdered and clergy and common folk were massacred with terrifyingly brutal vengeance. It has been estimated that as many souls perished in that West Country rebellion as were lost from the area in both World Wars combined.

Without a stable religion, superstitious fear of demons rose: one bishop wrote to Elizabeth I that 'witches and sorcerers within these last few years are marvellously increased within your grace's realm'. Sad to say, but many private feuds must have taken advantage of the witch-hunts as neighbour accused neighbour of muttered spells and dodgy gestures.

The regimented straight lines of Enclosure fields in North Yorkshire. (© Gillian Hovell)

Equally uncertain was the poor farmers' grip on the land. Despite a rash of legislation since Henry VII's time, vast tracts of land were still being cleared by private enclosures as sheep and cattle took the place not just of manpower-greedy arable land but of actual villagers too as the redundant land-workers were cast out of their homes to make way for fresh and more profitable pasture.

Excavations in Norwich confirm the scale of poverty in the land. The census organised in 1570 by the Burghers of the town reported that 20 per cent of the population was in urgent need. The monasteries and the guilds had once provided for the poor but now the Tudor Poor Laws of 1601 tried to cater for them and the whole nation was taxed to cover the cost. But each claimant had to be worthy or they received not a penny and 'sturdy beggars' were punished. In Scotland, those who could not justify a town's 'pauper's badge' were thrown out to starve. The suffering was made worse by disastrous harvests in the 1580s and '90s, followed by famine (1620-23) and the plague of 1665. Poverty equalled death.

For those with money though, the political, cultural and scientific revolutions of the seventeenth century created a boom time for cottage industries. The proliferation of guilds shows how everyone from glaziers to rope makers and tailors were on the up, and the mining and textile industries churned out more and more material as technical advances increased output. Disparking added to the climate of change: medieval hunting forests had displaced many villagers 400 years earlier and since then they had been static features in the landscape. Now the licences were removed and the entrepreneurial farmers and industrialists moved in.

All this change prompted folk to think for themselves and the Elizabethan Age enjoyed a cultural renaissance. Shakespeare led the way and poets like Edmund Spenser and John Milton scribed eternal truths about humanity while philosophers like Sir Thomas More embodied Sir Francis Bacon's aphorism, 'knowledge (*scientia*) is power'. Explorers of a different kind opened up the world to America and to all its fruits: tobacco, potatoes (later so crucial to starving populations) and the profits of slave trading were only some of the goodies on offer.

Everything was open to debate, even religion. Scotland went on to revel in her age of Enlightenment as reason was upheld as the means towards improvement, virtue and practical benefits for one and all. Robert Burns and Adam Smith were among the outstanding thinkers of their age. The nightmare of the Scottish clearances and the resulting mass emigrations carried these inspirations and achievements across to America.

In 1837, eighteen-year-old Victoria was crowned queen. She would rule for the next sixty-four years. During her reign, Britain would become the world's most powerful nation and a fifth of the world's map would turn pink, while relative peace and prosperity nearly doubled Britain's population.

While revolutions raged across Europe in the mid 1800s, Britain managed to hold its own relatively bloodless revolution: solid (if not aesthetically pleasing) almshouses, schools and hospitals were established in the towns which were rife with disease, polluted water and overcrowding. Jane Austin's rural society had been replaced, within a generation, by the life in the slums that Charles Dickens described. For the first time in history, the factory clock, not the rhythm of the seasons, regulated life.

Failure to pay your way in the new world resulted in the nightmare of the dark days of the workhouse. Here, families were divided, children were forced to work and abuse was rife, resulting in newspapers horrifying the nations with reports of inhuman scandals – Andover's inmates were found gnawing the bones they were meant to be crushing to make fertiliser, while the drunken workhouse manager abused the women. Outside the workhouse, execution, gaol and transportation were the unforgiving price of even the slightest crime.

Social reform was inevitable in a land where one in five children born alive died before the age of five. Cholera claimed 22,000 deaths in the first epidemic of 1831 alone, tuberculosis took 60,000 lives every decade of Victoria's reign, and the 'Great Stink' of 1858 even forced Parliament to close when the desperate measure of curtains soaked in chloride of lime failed to ease the stench from the polluted Thames. Cynics noted how sanitation and drainage were suddenly on the agenda and the Embankment and a new sewer system for London promptly planned. It was no coincidence that Wordsworth wrote so wistfully and lovingly of green landscapes in the 1840s.

At the same time, Scotland suffered from the potato famine, and the cruelty of the clearances continued – many fled to the lowland towns and northern England or emigrated. The failed potato crop in Ireland caused widespread famine and over a million people starved. Its population continued to drop throughout the Victorian Age, as emigration bled Ireland dry. The inequality of the Union's quality of life inevitably resulted in the 'Irish Question' as the cry for Home Rule grew louder.

Britain was ripe for reform. The People's Charter in 1838 had demanded more voting equality; the hated price-fixing Corn Acts and the resultant Anti Corn Law League in 1839 put a strain on law and order. Reform Acts multiplied and political debate was typified by the Gladstone-Disraeli duelling. Some issues began to sound very modern: one law even tried to fix a limit on MPs' expenses. Towards the end of the nineteenth century more and more new social laws were introduced, including growing workers' rights in Mines Acts and Factory Acts, and education for all (albeit thickly spread with Christian morals and a starting with just a few bare hours between slavish labour).

Life was speeding up. From 1830, the railway network raced across the land – by 1851, 6800 miles of track criss-crossed Britain and now, for the first time in history, you could travel faster than a galloping horse and goods could be carried with ease from town to town. Within thirty years, information gathering went from horseback to instant global news as the telegraph linked London to New York.

Science was seeking to explain the world and new theories and inventions tumbled over one another. In 1859, Darwin's *On the Origin of Species* even challenged the very concept of what it meant to be human. By the end of the century, the world must have seemed an ever-changing place. H.G. Wells' science fiction tales were satires and allegories on an uncertain future.

This watermill is just one of the rescued buildings at Weald and Downland Open Air Museum. (Reproduced with permission of the Weald and Downland Open Air Museum)

The World Wars dominated the first half of the twentieth century. The apparent timelessness of the countryside was about to end: weathered faces look out of 1920s photographs as they hand-reap the corn or walk behind horse-drawn ploughs in scenes that had barely changed for centuries. Quite suddenly, new machinery reduced the manpower needed and tore open the fields into open spaces: all that remained of the old way of life were a few preserved tools such as scythes, and the traces of the old smaller, man-manageable field systems. A new world was beginning.

Things to do

Capturing the essence of 500 years isn't easy but at Geffrye Museum in Kingsland Road, London they manage it very neatly: take a compressed journey through time, seeing how life at home changed as you walk through rooms from 1600s to the present day. Larger scale versions exist at Chiltern Open Air Museum at Chalfont St Giles (Buckinghamshire), St Fagan's Rural Museum in South Wales and Kingussie's Open Air Rural Museum in Scotland – there you step inside and walk around rescued buildings from other times.

For a selection of rural industrial buildings, head for the open air Weald and Downland Museum again – it's not just home to medieval houses. You can see early industrial workshops such as a rescued and working seventeenth-century watermill (with later additions) in action as it grinds flour, a horse 'gin' used to pump water from wells and mines, a timber-built brick-drying shed, a working forge from 1900, and a seventeenth-century barn housing exhibits on plumbing, stone masons and glaziers. Step back in time as you try some Tudor style food, meet traditional livestock, and enjoy their regular demonstrations of crafts and skills. Why not take a virtual tour at www.wealdow.co.uk before you go?

Telford's Ironbridge Gorge is a must if you want to capture the scale of the innovations that launched us into our Industrial Age. Abraham Darby's brooding furnace is where it all began. The Iron Bridge spans 100ft across the Severn River and towers 45ft above the gorge.

For the story of how the railways spread across Britain, visit the largest railway museum in the world at the National Railway Museum in York. Go to www.nrm.org.uk for more details.

To follow the breathtaking discoveries that have changed our lives, visit any science museum – the large ones are scattered across our cities (Manchester's Science Museum, London's Science Museum and Kew Bridge Steam Museum are amongst the biggest).

The value of Scotland's industrial heritage was shown when Lady Victoria Colliery in Newtongrange, Midlothian, was recently named Scotland's 'most treasured place'. Opened in the 1890s it was only closed down in 1981 and was one of the first Scottish 'super-pits' employing almost 2000 men. It now houses the 5-star visitor attraction, the Scottish Mining Museum. It has exhibitions, a hands-on operation centre, pithead, re-created underground roadway and coalface experience, working winding engine (the largest in Scotland), audio-visual shows and tours – there's so much to see that your ticket allows you three visits during the next year so you don't have to miss anything.

If you're in Wales, the World Heritage Site, Blaenavon Industrial Landscape, shows the harsh realities of coal and iron mining in the nineteenth century. Explore the quarries, mines, furnaces, houses, public buildings and early railway system that made up this industrial landscape.

Life in Britain was transformed in the Victorian era. York Castle Museum has a replica Victorian street. First created in 1938 it's had a whole new revamp and is full of new, inspirational features that draw the visitor into the atmosphere.

Yesterday's World at Battle in East Sussex will assault your senses with sounds and smells of a hundred years from the Victorian world through time, right through to the 1950s.

Get behind the scenes of the decision makers of the Second World War at Churchill Museum and Cabinet War Rooms in London. The Imperial War Museum in London is the central archive and repository for all things military – don't miss it.

Duxford, near Cambridge, was one of the earliest RAF stations. Begun in 1917 as a pilot training centre, it became a fighter station in 1924 and played a key role in the Battle of Britain. It now houses the Imperial War Museum's world-famous collection of aircraft. Of course there are several air shows a year around the country – catch one and you might get to see the last flying Second World War aircraft in action.

York Cold War Bunker was equipped to monitor nuclear explosions and fallout in Yorkshire between 1961 until as recently as 1991. Decontamination rooms and original fittings combine with a guided tour and short PG-rated film to make this a thought-provoking visit.

Eden Camp at Malton in North Yorkshire was a POW camp which is now a museum dedicated to 'The People's War 1939-45'.

Trawl through local newspapers from the war years to get first-hand evidence which brings the archaeology to life.

Reading up

Books on the Tudors weigh down the shelves and they range from highly academic (*The Oxford History of England* volumes from the year dot to the twentieth century) to children's books (never underestimate the use of a children's book as a means to gain a quick impression of the facts!).

The thinkers of the Elizabethan cultural boom wrote reams that can tell us about the mindset of the time: try a taste of Shakespeare or the poets John Donne and Edmund Spenser to set the scene.

Simon Schama's *A History of Britain: British Wars 1603-1776* traces nearly two centuries of troubled years while *A History of Britain III: the Fate of Empire 1776-2001* charts the remorseless march of progress through the industrial revolution to our own day (BBC Books 2003).

Watch Andrew Marr's BBC series, *Britain from Above* which includes his penultimate episode in which the hard industrial landscape of Britain is seen to vanish almost before our eyes.

The literature of a time tells us much about the aspirations, hope and dreams of the folk who lived then. Compare Jane Austin's 1810 rural society with Charles Dickens' revelations about life in the slums of London just forty years later. Follow Daphne Du Maurier's family saga, *Hungry Hill* as it captures the social changes, generation by generation from the dawn of capitalist coal mining up to the early twentieth century. Or sample the uncertainty of the changing times at the end of the nineteenth century by opening the pages of H.G. Wells' satirical science fiction books *The Time Machine* and *War of the Worlds.*

There are many books about the World Wars. Archaeology-based ones include Nicholas J. Saunders' *Killing Time: Archaeology and the First World War* (The History Press Ltd 2007) and Andrew Robertshaw and David Kenyon's *Digging the Trenches* (Pen & Sword Military 2008)

Personal accounts of the war are powerful ways to gain an insight into the realities behind the archaeology: *Tommy's War: A First World War Diary 1913-1918* by Thomas Cairns Livingstone and Andrew Marr (Harperpress 2008) and *Home in Time for*

Breakfast: A First World War Diary by Stuart Chapman (Athena Press 2007) are good starting points.

B. Lowry's *20th Century Defences in Britain: An Introductory Guide* gives a straight account of the state of our tattered remains from the World Wars (CBA Practical Handbooks in Archaeology 12, 1995).

Photographs are a valuable primary source for archaeologists. You can find them in books like Richard Holmes' *World War II in Photographs* (Carlton Books 2000) or check that attic for forgotten mementos.

PART THREE

Digging Deeper

KIT CHECK

We can often spot archaeology as we go about our day-to-day activities, but sometimes we need to head out into the hills and moorlands to experience the more remote monuments like stone circles and ancient field boundaries. When heading out into these more rugged terrains, we need to follow some fundamental hikers' rules:

☞ **Take plenty of drinks and snacks** – you need to be able to keep your energy levels up and to boost them from time to time. Ruins are great places for picnics anyway!

☞ **Don't be a mountain rescue statistic:** know where you're going and plan how to get there before you set out – use a walker's map, keep to the footpaths and allow plenty of time to get there, be distracted by the archaeology for longer than you expect, and get back again.

Dressed for action (© Janis Heward)

TOP TIP

ENJOY THE WEATHER!

Archaeologists get outside in every season: crop marks in a field show up during hot dry summers while a frosting of snow and/or in a low winter's sun show up the subtle but often different lumps and bumps in the same field. But getting out there means facing the weather – and it's notorious in Britain for changing in a moment. Always wear decent footwear and put an extra layer and waterproofs in your pack. Then even the most atmospheric weather can be enjoyable (*colour plate 32*).

If you haven't got a hat, get one or borrow one! Archaeologists are renowned for wearing daft hats for several good reasons: they keep the sun off; they keep the rain off; they keep the snow and hail off too; they shield your eyes from the low sun that is so useful for seeing grassy lumps and bumps; and they keep you surprisingly warm when it's cold (and cooler when it's hot).

However, if the weather's just too foul out there, don't despair – it's a good day for a spot of indoor research with maps old and new, aerial photos and old photos, background reading or even document hunting in record offices.

BASIC FIELDCRAFT

Never forget that you're on someone else's land. Be polite and considerate to landowners and share your thoughts and discoveries with them. For safety's sake, go exploring with a friend whenever possible – sprained ankles and the occasional iffy reception are both risks best dealt with in company.

Take care on sites – some require a certain element of nimbleness to access them, as demonstrated by the author at Lligwy Chamber. (© Mark Hovell)

DO'S AND DON'TS

Don't ...

✗ trample on crops – they are a farmer's livelihood.

✗ enter fields with bulls or cows and calves, especially if you have a dog with you.

✗ scare the animals.

✗ climb on boundary walls – stand on stiles if you need a better view.

✗ leave litter – take it home with you.

✗ Never pick up or move stones, dig holes or light fires.

Do ...

✓ always check you have free access (land ownership and rights of way can change) – keep to the public footpaths unless it is open access or you have explicit permission to explore.

✓ respect seasonal constraints on access: lambing, game bird rearing and shooting seasons.

✓ keep your dog under close control – a dog seen worrying sheep can be shot.

✓ always leave gates as you found them.

✓ park thoughtfully, without blocking gateways or tracks.

TO DIG OR NOT TO DIG?

Not really a question at all: the simple answer is 'don't'. There's no need to – archaeology is evident all around us. However, if a site is screaming for further exploration and you have access and permission from the landowner, hunt out a local archaeology group who have a tame professional archaeologist in tow. They have the know-how, the insurance and the kit to help you to really explore the site and get the best out of it without harming the archaeology.

Keep to the public rights of way.
(© Gillian Hovell)

METAL DETECTORS

All good harmless fun on the unstratified ever-shifting sands of a beach or the disturbed topsoil of ploughed fields, and they're great tools in checking a *bona fide* dig,

but ...

- if you take a detector into a field and then simply dig up your bit of metal without recording its grid reference, soil layers and 'context' no one will ever be able to tell whether it from a burial, a battlefield or a workshop or just a stray find – all the information that artefact could tell us is lost forever. To be worth doing, unearthing finds needs to follow the rules:
- If you really must use a metal detector, do so with a reputable group who have official and professional archaeological connections and advice. Many work alongside archaeologists, checking spoil heaps and identifying hot spots.

TOP TIP

THE RULES

The National Council for Metal Detecting has a rigorous Code of Conduct which can be found on www.ncmd.co.uk. You should especially note that:

- You must always get permission from the landowner (and occupier of the land if this is different from the owner) – not doing so may result in criminal charge and you may be sued for damages.
- Scheduled Ancient Monuments are protected by law. No one can use a metal detector on these without written agreement of the Secretary of State. So don't even think it.
- It is an offence to remove archaeological objects using a metal detector from a scheduled site or an Area of Archaeological Importance (and in England this rule cover all areas of historic towns too, York, Exeter etc).
- Scottish law requires that all finds be reported.
- Some local authorities have by-laws which forbid metal detecting on their land.
- The Treasure Act of 1996 requires reporting of certain categories of finds.
- You must call the police and notify the landowner if you find any live explosives.

MAKING A DIFFERENCE: RECORDING AND REPORTING

So you've found some fascinating archaeology and you want to describe it. What do you need to do? Firstly, remember that anyone can make a special discovery or notice a link others have never seen before – and this feature might be your big moment, so it's worth doing the job properly. Always take along a couple of extra goodies with you:

- A camera is a must. Being able to record what you see so you can compare it with other examples of similar features elsewhere boosts the learning curve immensely. See the section below on how to make the most of your photographic skills.
- Pop a notepad in your pocket – it's better than scribbling notes on scraps of paper which can be lost so easily. You can even buy waterproof notebooks now so that, should the heavens open or you drop it in a stream, you don't end up bringing back a lump of mushy papier maché. Take a waterproof pen too – otherwise known as a pencil.
- A compass is useful – for more than just finding your way home again, as we shall find out below.

But just how do we record archaeology?

Making a record
- Take photographs.
- Make notes. These should include:

A description of the feature. Is it, for example, a level platform, circular mound, linear ditch, standing stone or recumbent stone …

The feature's location. If you can, note its map reference: if you have a whizzy hikers' gadget called a GPS (Global Positioning System), you can use that to record it; failing that, find where you are on a large scale map, work out the grid reference if you can or else you can resort to the time-honoured 'x' marks the spot on the map. If you don't do any of these, you'll never remember which of the ten fields you walked through had that interesting stone in it …

Describe the location: is it in a grassy field, a boulder strewn hillside, rough pasture, moorland, deciduous woodland, etc. Also, which 'way' does it face: is it on a gently sloping south-facing hill, or on eastern shoulder of hill, on the west side of river, or is that linear mound facing east-west, etc.

Roughly measure the feature. If you don't have a tape measure or ruler handy, guess. If it's big, pace it out with strides (one large stride is approximately 1 metre).

Be brave: write down what you think it is – saying it might be a Bronze Age burial mound or a charcoal clamp gives a good impression of what it looks like. It helps to give your reasons for this calculated guess: its size, shape, other nearby features, fragments of charcoal in rabbit scratchings … etc.

Last, but not least, note the date of your site visit.

Leave space to add other notes later: is your feature marked on the OS map already? Is it on old maps (look up www.old-maps.co.uk) and if so, which ones? Is it on an aerial photograph (try google maps, 'satellite' mode)? Is it mentioned in any books?

TOP TIP

PHOTOGRAPHY: TAKING YOUR PIC

It doesn't matter whether you use a digital or traditional camera. A decent zoom is invaluable though: you can't always get close to a monument – it can be fenced off or the footpath simply doesn't go near it. Don't trespass – use the zoom instead.

If possible, photograph your feature 'straight on', not at an angle, so you get an undistorted view.

Photograph it from each side. And, if you have a compass or you can tell roughly from where the sun is, make a note of which way – north, south, east or west – you were facing each time. You'd be amazed at how confusing the pictures are if you don't.

On at least one shot, add something as a 'scale' so you can tell if it's 6cm or 6m long. Choose one appropriate to the size of the feature: a coin for tiny ones, a ruler for bigger ones and your best mate for the ones big enough walk around.

Do add a few 'angled' shots for emphasis, depth, artistic mood etc., but don't use these as your only record.

Take shots of 'details' (the cup-and-ring carving, or a inscription, etc.) but also take one that shows the detail in the context of the whole feature plus a shot of it in its surroundings (so you can remember where it was).

Many cameras have a 'macro' setting for close-ups: make use of it.

Beware the single stray grass stem in front of your detail shot – the camera will focus on that, not the interesting feature behind.

Watch for unwanted shadows – your own, your friend's or that of nearby trees or structures.

However, low sunlight is really useful for emphasising the lumps and bumps of earthworks.

If the light is poor, experiment with the flash, fill-in flash, or aperture settings – digital cameras often have various pre-set options you could try ones such as 'sunny' or 'cloudy' or a menu with options such as 'available light' on it.

Always check your digital picture before moving on – believe me, it's peeving to get home and find it out of focus when you could have had a second or even third attempt.

And always make a note of what you've photographed – either in your notebook there and then, or that evening when you get home and look through what you've taken. Months on, you can't always remember where that rock was or why you photographed that bump. An unidentified photograph is useless to anyone else, or even to yourself in six month's time.

Photographs are vital records. (© Jim Brophy)

Sketching

A picture can paint a thousand words. Making a quick sketch of the feature and its relation to other features (like walls) is invaluable. This can be a simple line drawing that even the least artistic can do. Or you can do it the archaeological way and make a sketch survey which will show details that no amount of photography or writing can reveal.

This is the technique you see in archaeology books where little 'tadpoles' mark earthwork slopes. The thicker end represents more soil (higher ground) and the thin end is the bottom of the slope (with less soil equalling less pencil marking). So, depending on which end is thicker, a circle of hachure marks represents a circular pit (if the thicker ends are on the outside) or a circular mound (if the thicker ends are on the inside). Also, the closer the hachure marks are to each other, the steeper the slope is – just a few marks mean the slope is gentle while sardine-style marks mean

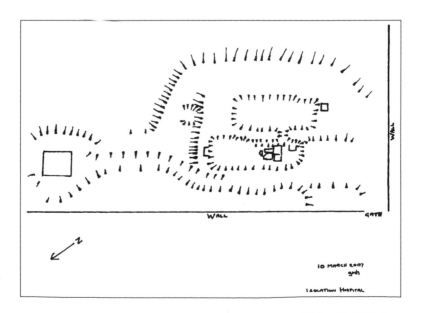

A rough sketch survey like this, with hachure marks showing even low earthwork mounds, can give a valuable impression of the site – this one is an old, long gone isolation hospital in North Yorkshire. (© Gillian Hovell)

it's virtually unwalkable on. And pure vertical drops are shown by 'tail-less' hachure marks, i.e. stumpy triangles. All that's left then is to add a compass point to show which way up the sketch is and to label your sketch with the feature's name, its location (grid reference), the date of the sketch and your name.

Just give it a go. It's a peaceful and absorbing occupation and it has the added advantage that it makes you really look closely at what you're drawing. You'll get to see details you wouldn't otherwise notice.

WHO TO TELL

If you think you've found something new, your first port of call must be the landowner (if the feature is on private land). Then contact the Historic Environment Officer at your local council's Heritage and Environment section to see if it's been reported before, or contact your nearest Portable Antiquities Scheme (PAS) officer (via www.finds.org.uk).

Remember: a responsible approach to archaeology is crucial if others are to enjoy and benefit from it too. And, who knows, you might become a local 'expert' on the features near you – maybe even making a great discovery. Archaeology isn't just for the academics and the television presenters – it's for all of us and we can all enjoy it and even help to discover it.

A HELPING HAND

Anyone can visit the past but we all have to be taught certain skills and be given top tips to know what it is we're looking for and how to understand what we're looking at. There are many ways you can get help:

- Site guides and signboards: the guidebooks and notices at any official sites have masses of research compressed into manageable portions – they're a wonderful resource we can tap into.
- Museums and their staff: national museums give you the big picture, but visit local museums for a taste of the area you're exploring. Each region has its own unique stories from the past. And these local museums are often staffed by volunteers who are keen to chat and share their enthusiasm with you.
- National societies: to find out more about particular historical sites, contact the owners or guardians. The major heritage organisations are:
- English Heritage (www.english-heritage.org.uk) is the leading government agency for managing England's historic buildings and archaeological heritage. Membership gives free admission to their sites.
- The National Trust for England, Wales and Northern Ireland (www.nationaltrust. org.uk), and the National Trust for Scotland (www.nts.org.uk) now own many sites across our islands. Members have free access to all their properties.

- CADW is the historic environment service of the Welsh Assembly Government and it maintains many wonderful sites in Wales. In case you're wondering, Cadw (pronounced cad-oo) is a Welsh word meaning 'to keep'.
- National Databases: County Record Offices are there for you to use. Register with them in person, just as you would for a normal library. Don't be shy about approaching staff in these unfamiliar places – everyone who has ever visited a Record Office has asked for help!
- The National Archives have a truly fantastic website (www.nationalarchives.gov. uk) that gives you access to a huge variety of historical documents. Click on 'Search Archives' or enter their A2A ('Access to Archives') pages and prepare to spend the next several hours going on a incredible voyage of discovery.
- British History Online (www.british-history.ac.uk) has searchable copies of historical sources including the Victoria County History which explores counties in detail, certain local records and, crucially, old Ordnance Survey Maps you can view.

TOP TIP

Always consider the following when using primary sources, e.g. documents, maps, letters, i.e. anything original rather than 'reported' or 'interpreted' fact: when was it made, who made it, why did they make it and who did them make it for? Just because it's original doesn't mean it was an unbiased viewpoint!

BOOKS

Libraries, book shops (including those on sites), websites, and friends' bookshelves are all good sources for reading material. General overviews include the classic reference book, *The Handbook of British Archaeology* by Lesley Adkins and Roy A. Adkins (Constable, 1998) while *Archaeology: A Very Short Introduction* by Paul G. Bahn (Oxford University Press, 2000) is a witty and informative look at worldwide archaeology from the year dot. Check out the specialist publishers' catalogues too – The History Press is just one of them. A few relevant titles from them are:

Unravelling the Landscape: An Inquisitive Approach to Archaeology, edited by Mark Bowden (1999) and *Be Your own landscape detective: Investigating where you are* by Richard Muir (2007) can help you to look closer at the history around you.

Victor Ambrus' (of *Time Team* fame) *Drawing on Archaeology: Bringing History Back to Life* (2006) is full of depictions of just what life might have been like through the ages.

Books like *Environmental Archaeology: Principles and Methods* by Terry O'Connor (2005) can take you into the realms of virtually any specialist area of archaeology. If the study of bones or pottery or particular eras inspires you, there'll be a book just for you ...

MAGAZINES

Current magazines to help you to dig deeper into archaeology are:

British Archaeology, the CBA's magazine.

Current Archaeology and, for those wanting a bigger view, *Current World Archaeology*.

Antiquity is a quarterly magazine for those with a serious interest in archaeology. Subscribe via their website, www.antiquity.ac.uk.

There are also a selection of history-based magazines, such as BBC's *History* and *Who do you think you are?*, *History Today,* and *Heritage*.

THE INTERNET

Use internet search engines to look for official websites on particular sites. Check out the national organisations such as English Heritage as they often provide reams of historical and 'how to' information. Stick to these authoritative websites at first, until you can recognise when good solid facts or 'approved' theories are being set out – be warned that there are many 'personal opinions' and 'wild ideas' out there.

TOP TIP

TRY THESE THREE...

Scotland's Rural Past (SRP) is a national project supporting Scottish local communities as they investigate deserted rural settlements. Follow the menu on their website www.scotlandsruralpast.org for clear, easy to follow guidelines that can help you whatever your archaeological area of interest – they cover everything from 'Getting going', 'Doing research' and 'Doing fieldwork' to specifics such as 'Recording / Digital images' and a glossary of terms.

If you can face the formal archaeologists' lingo, a detailed description of just about every type of archaeological feature you're ever likely to find is available in the English Heritage's 'Monument Class Descriptions' on www.eng-h.gov.uk/mpp/mcd (or put monument class descriptions into a search engine).

Straight, no-nonsense summaries of historical eras can be found on the BBC's website – just type your particular era or topic and 'history' into the search facility.

TELEVISION AND RADIO

The quality of factual history and archaeology programmes in the media is astonishing. Whole series and one-off programmes can open up whole new areas of history in a user-friendly way – enjoy them!

JOINING UP: GETTING INVOLVED

If you want to get more involved, or even excavate, get in touch with one or more of the following:

Major national archaeological societies include:

- The Council for British Archaeology (CBA) is an independent charity working towards advancing archaeology in Great Britain and Northern Ireland. Members receive their magazine, British Archaeology which is well worth reading. www.yac@britarch.ac.uk. Don't forget to look out for their National Archaeological Week events in July every year.

- The Council for Scottish Archaeology (CSA) has compiled a comprehensive guide to identifying different archaeological features which can be downloaded from www.scottisharchaeology.org.uk.

- The Royal Archaeological Institute plays a leading role in sharing and promoting research in archaeology and history through its Archaeological Journal, meetings and field trips. See more about them on www.royalarchaeolinst.org.

- Many independent archaeological sites actively encourage the general public to take part, either as diggers, guides, assistants or as 'Friends of ....'. You too can be there at the sharp end of archaeology.

- Local clubs and societies: archaeology is a chance to discover new skills and make new friends in the process: members of local heritage groups will happily share their wide-ranging skills with you. A fellow member with a smattering of botany can tell you how a particular plant can show you what's under the soil – it might be boggy here but dry over there: is archaeology the reason? A grain of geology know-how, on the other hand, is a rock-solid foundation for knowing what resources could have been mined or grown on a certain hillside. www.local-history.co.uk includes links to dozens of local societies and information sources.

Local history events like this Iron-Age (Nidderdale) Project walk take place throughout the British Isles and are great places to meet the local heritage and archaeology groups. (© Gillian Hovell)

Some essential digging kit. (© Gillian Hovell)

- The www.britarch.ac.uk/info/socs pages of the CBA's website provide links to a mass of regional and local societies as well as to helpful archaeology information and news.
- Local adult education courses often include Archaeology, Heritage or Local History sessions to which all are welcome. Many universities offer similar extra-mural courses and mature students are as welcome as school leavers to join their major courses.
- Or you could take a more relaxed approach and go on a holiday that tours archaeology sites and museums. Put something like 'archaeology tours' into an internet search engine and see if you like the sound of any of them!

So why not get out there and enjoy visiting the past!

BIBLIOGRAPHY

Adkins, Lesley & Adkins, Roy A., *The Handbook of British Archaeology* (Constable 1998)

Alcock, Joan P., *Life in Roman Britain* (Tempus Publishing Ltd 2006)

Aldhouse-Green, Stephen, 'Great Sites: Paviland Cave' (*British Archaeology* Issue 61, October 2001)

Allen J. Romilly and Anderson Joseph, *The Early Christian Monuments of Scotland* (Pinkfoot Press 1993)

Ambrus, Victor, *Drawing on Archaeology: Bringing History Back to Life* (Tempus Publishing Ltd 2006)

Ashmore P.J., *Bronze Age Scotland* (Historic Scotland/Trafalgar Square 1997)

Ashmore, P. *Maes Howe* (Historic Scotland 1993)

Bahn, Paul G., *Archaeology: A Very Short Introduction* (Oxford University Press 2000)

Barton, Nicholas, *Stone Age Britain* (English Heritage/Batsford 1997)

Bede, *Ecclesiastical History of the English People* (translated by Latham, R.E., Penguin Classics 1990)

Beresford Ellis, P., *A Guide to Early Celtic Remains in Britain* (Constable 1991)

Bewley, Bob, *Prehistoric Settlements* (Batsford/English Heritage 1994)

Blair, John, *The Anglo-Saxon Age: A Very Short Introduction* (Oxford Paperbacks)

Bowden, Mark (ed.) *Unravelling the landscape: An Inquisitive Approach to Archaeology* (Tempus Publishing Ltd 1999)

Breeze, David & Dobson, Brian, *Hadrian's Wall* (Penguin 1997)

Breeze, David, *Roman Forts in Britain* (Shire Archaeology 1983)

Brophy, J. *Nidderdale Iron: A Forgotten Industry* (Howber 2005)

Brophy, Kenneth, 'Seeing the Cursus as a Symbolic River' (*British Archaeology* Issue no 44, May 1999)

Caesar, Julius, *The Conquest of Gaul* (translated by Handford, S.A., Penguin Classics 1979)

Cairns Livingstone, Thomas, & Marr, Andrew, *Tommy's War: A First World War Diary* (HarperPress 2008)

Campbell, Ewarn, 'Excavations of a wheelhouse and other Iron Age structures at Sollas, North Uist by RJC Atkinson in 1957' (ProcSoc Antiq Scot, 121 (1991), 117-173, fiches 1: D1-3. F10)

Chapman, Stuart, *Home in Time for Breakfast: A First World War Diary* (Athena Press 2007)

Clarke, David, *Skara Brae* (Historic Scotland 1989)

Crow, Jim, *Housesteads* (Batsford / English Heritage 1995)

Courtlandt Canby (sic). *A Guide to the Archaeological sites of the Birtish Isles* (Hudson Group 1988)

Cunliffe, Barry, *The Ancient Celts* (Penguin 1999)

Cunliffe, Barry, *Danebury* (English Heritage/Batsford)

Cunliffe, Barry W., *Iron Age Communities in Britain* (Routledge, 1991)

Cunliffe, Barry W., *Iron Age Britain* (Batsford/English Heritage 2004)

Cunlifee, Barry, *The Oxford Illustrated History of Prehistoric Europe* (2001)

Cunlifee, Barry, *Prehistoric Europe* (Oxford University Press 1994)

Darvill Timothy, Stamper Paul & Timby Jane, *England, An Archaeological Guide*, (OUP 2002)

English Heritage: *Monument Class Descriptions*, Various authors and dates

Darvill, Prof. T.C. *Prehistoric Britain* (Routledge 1998)

Darvill T.C. *Prehistoric Britain from the Air* (Cambridge University Press 1996)

de la Bédoyère, Guy, *Roman Britain: A New History* (Thames & Hudson 2006)

de la Bédoyère, Guy, *The Finds of Roman Britain* (Batsford 1988

Dyer, J. *Discovering Archaeology in England and Wales* (Shire 1997)

English Heritage, *Twentieth-Century Military Sites: Current approaches to their recording and conservation* (English Heritage 2003)

Evans Estyn, *Prehistoric and Early Christian Ireland, A Guide* (Batsford 1966)

Fawcett, Richard, *Scottish Cathedrals* (Batsford/Historic Scotland 1997)

Gillingham, John and Griffiths, Ralph, *Medieval Britain: A Very Short Introduction* (Oxford Paperbacks)

Hall, David, 'Medieval Fields in their Many Forms' (*British Archaeology*, Issue 33, April 1998)

du Maurier, Daphne, *Hungry Hill* (Gollancz 1943)

Hinton, David, *Archaeology, Economy and Society* (Routledge 1990)

Holmes, Richard, *World War II in Photographs* (Carlton Books 2000)

Hoskins, W.G. *The Making of the English Landscape*, (Guild Publishing 1988)

Ireland, Stanley, *Roman Britain: A Sourcebook* (Routledge 2nd edition, 1996)

James, Simon, *Archaeology in Britain: New Views of the Past* (British Museum 1986)

James, Simon & Rigby, Valerie, *Britain and the Celtic Iron Age* (British Museum)

Johnson, David, *Roman Villas* (Shire Archaeology 1983)

Jones Duncan, *The Pocket Scottish History series A Wee Guide to The Picts* (Goblinshead 1998)

Kipling, Rudyard, *Puck of Pook's Hill* (Peguin Classics 1995)

Lacey Robert & Danziger Danny, *The Year 1000: What Life was Like At the Turn of the First Millennium* (Little, Brown & company, 1999)

Lane, Alan, 'Citadel of the first Scots' (*British Archaeology*, Issue 62, Dec 2001 CBA)

Legge A.J. and Rowley-Conwy P.A., *Star Carr Revisited* (University College London 1988)

Lowry, B., *20th Century Defences in Britain: An Introductory Guide* (CBA, 1995)

Marsden, Barry, *Exploring Prehistoric and Roman Britain* (Greenlight, 2003)

McOrmish, David, 'Cursus: Solving a 6,000 year old puzzle', British Archaeology, Issue 69, March 2003.

Millett, Martin, *Roman Britain* (Batsford / English Heritage 2005)

Muir, Richard, *Be Your Own Landscape Detective: investigating where you are* (The History Press 2007)

Noonan, Damien, *Castles and Ancient Monuments of England* (Aurum 1999)

Noonian, Damien, *Castles and Ancient Monuments of Scotland* (Aurum 2000)

Ottaway, Patrick, *Archaeology in British Towns: From the Emperor Claudius to the Black Death* (Routledge, 1992)

Palsson, Hermann and Edwards, Paul, *The Orkneyinga Saga* (Penguin Classics 1978)

Parfitt, Simon, 'Pakefield: a weekend to remember', British Archaeology, Issue 86, Jan/Feb 2006 (CBA)

Pargetter, Edith, *The Brothers of Gwynedd*

Parker Pearson, Michael, *Bronze Age Britain* (English Heritage/Batsford 2005)

Peddie, John, *Conquest: The Roman Invasion* (The History Press 2005)

Pitts, Michael and Roberts, Mark, *Fairweather Eden* (Century 1977)

Platt, Colin, *The English Medieval Town* (Secker and Warburg 1976)

Pollard, Joshua, *Neolithic Britain* (Shire Archaeology 1997)

Pollard, Justin, *Seven Ages of Britain* (Hodder & Stoughton 2003)

Pound, N.J.G., *The Medieval Castle* (Leicester University Press, 1990)

Pryor, Francis, *Britain BC: Life in Britain and Ireland before the Romans* (Harper Perenniall 2004)

Pryor, Francis, *Farmers in Prehistoric Britain* (Tempus Publishing Ltd 1998)

Pryor, Francis, *Britain AD: A Quest for Arthur, England and the Anglo-Saxons* (HarperCollins)

Quinney, Anthony, *The Traditional Buildings of England* (Thames and Hudson 1990)

Ramsey, Nigel, *English Medieval Industries* (Hambledon Press 1991)

Renfrew, Colin, *Prehistory: Making of the Human Mind* (W&N 2007)

Richards, Julian D., *The Vikings: A Very Short Introduction* (Oxford Paperbacks 2005)

Rippon, Stephen, *Historic Landscape Analysis: Deciphering the Countryside* (Council for British Archaeology 2004)

Ritchie, Annie, *Prehistoric Orkney* (Historic Scotland/Batsford 1995)

Robertshaw, Andrew & Kenyon, David, *Digging the Trenches* (Pen & Sword Military 2008)

Roe, Errek, *The Lower and Middle Palaeolithic Periods in Britain* (Routledge 1981)

Salway, Peter, *Roman Britain: A Very Short Introduction* (Oxford Paperbacks 2000)

Saunders, Nicholas J., *Killing Time: Archaeology and the First World War* (The History Press 2007)

Scarre Chris, *The Megalithic Monuments of Britain and Ireland* (Thames & Hudson 2007)

Schama, Simon, *A History of Britain: At the Edge of the World? 3000 BC–AD 1603* (BBC 2000)

Schama, Simon, *A History of Britain: British Wars 1603-1776* (BBC 2003)

Schama, Simon, *A History of Britain III: The Fate of Empire 1776-2001* (BBC 2003)

Smith, Christopher, *Late Stone Age Hunters of the British Isles* (Routledge 1992)

Steane, John, *The Archaeology of Medieval England and Wales* (Croom Helm 1984)

Stringer, Chris, Homo Britannicus: *The Incredible Story of Human Life in Britain* (Allen Lane 2007)

Sutcliff, Rosemary, *The Eagle of the Ninth* (Puffin 1977)

Tabraham, Chris, *Scottish Castles* (Batsford/Historic Scotland 1997)

Tacitus, *The Agricola* (Translated by Mattingly H., Penguin Classics 1980)

Thomas, Julian, *Understanding the Neolithic* (Routledge 1999)

Thomas, Roger J.C., 'POW Camps: What survives Where', (*The Archaeology of Conflict,* English Heritage Conservation Bulletin 44 June 2003)

Warren, Graeme, *Mesolithic Lives in Scotland* (Tempus Publishing Ltd 2005)

Wickham-Jones, Caroline, *Scotland's First Settlers* (Batsford/Historic Scotland 1994)

Wells, H.G. *The Time Machine* (Baronet 1995)

Wood, Eric S., *Collins Field Guide to Archaeology in Britain* (Collins 1963)

Wood, Michael, *Domesday: A Search for the Roots of England* (BBC Publications 1986)

Wood, Michael, *In Search of the Dark Ages* (BBC 2005)

Mark Whyman & Andy J Howard, *Archaeology and Landscape in the Vale of York* (York Archaeological Trust 2005)

Wymer, John, *Mesolithic Britain* (Shire Archaeology 1991)

Yeoman, Peter, *Medieval Scotland* (Batsford/Historic Scotland 1995)

INDEX

Page references in italics refer to black and white images. References in italic and **bold** refer to colour plates.

Visit our website and discover thousands of other History Press books.
www.thehistorypress.co.uk